Memory Lane...

# Surrey

Inspired by photographs from The Francis Frith Collection®

The Francis Frith Collection®

# Memory Lane...
# Surrey

THE FRANCIS FRITH COLLECTION

www.francisfrith.com

First published in the United Kingdom in 2012
by The Francis Frith Collection®

Paperback edition 2012 ISBN 978-1-84589-706-2



British Library Cataloguing in Publication Data

Memory Lane - Surrey

The Francis Frith Collection®
Oakley Business Park, Wylye Road,
Dinton, Wiltshire SP3 5EU
Tel: +44 (0) 1722 716 376
Email: info@francisfrith.co.uk
www.francisfrith.com

Printed and bound in Great Britain
Contains material sourced from responsibly managed forests

Front Cover: **NEWDIGATE, SIX BELLS 1924** 73521t
Frontispiece: **MERROW, THE FORGE 1913** 65231p



*The colour-tinting in this book is for illustrative purposes only, and is not intended to be historically accurate*

AS WITH ANY HISTORICAL DATABASE, THE FRANCIS FRITH ARCHIVE IS CONSTANTLY BEING CORRECTED AND IMPROVED, AND THE PUBLISHERS WOULD WELCOME INFORMATION ON OMISSIONS OR INACCURACIES

# Memory Lane – A Dedication

**This book has been compiled from a selection of the thousands of personal memories added by visitors to the Frith website and could not have happened without these contributions. We are very grateful to everyone who has taken the time to share their memories in this way. The combination of all these personal stories provides a wonderful insight into British life and this book is therefore dedicated to everyone who has taken the time to participate in the Frith Memories project.**

Each memory is personal to the writer yet the pictures painted are part of a shared inheritance, reminders of a life that so many people still cherish in their memories. For others, these memories will provide an insight into a way of life that has now vanished.

In the current uncertain times it is comforting to find so many stories full of human warmth which bring back happy memories of "the good old days". We hope that everyone reading this book will find stories that amuse and fascinate whilst at the same time be reminded of why we feel affection for Britain and what makes us all British.

Francis Frith always expressed the wish that his photographs be made available to as wide an audience as possible and so it is particularly pleasing to me that by creating the Frith web site we have been able to make this nationally important photographic record of Britain available to a worldwide audience. Now, by providing the Share Your Memories feature on the website we are delighted to provide an opportunity for members of the public to record their own stories and to see them published (both on the website and in this book), ensuring that they are shared and not lost or forgotten.

We hope that you too will be motivated to visit our website and add your own memories to this growing treasure trove – helping us to make it an even more comprehensive record of the changes that have taken place in Britain in the last 100 years and a resource that will be valued by generations to come.

John M Buck
Managing Director

www.francisfrith.com

# Cards, cornettos and the cage

If you hadn't fallen in the pond, you were not from Lingfield! So says my dad. The building to the right of the Cage (the name for the old village prison) in this photo was a shop. My memory of this shop only goes back to the mid 1970s. My grandparents' house was behind the shop (the hedge to the right on this photo is the edge of their property), and whilst on holiday visiting them, my brother and I would play cards with Granddad for 5p a hand. He always claimed that he 'was the best pontoon player in the world' although he would always twist on 18+! We always managed to win and when we both got up to 50p we would always run down the garden path and go to the shop and buy a Cornetto. My dad was born in the house and we would go back every 2 or 3 years but now my grandparents are both gone and these photos are great memories. During the late 1970s in the punk era a load of punks used to congregate around the Cage. One time my nan had had enough of the noise of them and their bikes, so she threw a bucket of water over one of them. They rode off and my nan made the front page of the East Grinstead Courier. She sent the paper over to us and I ran across the road and showed my auntie from my mother's side. I got a chocolate because we were a brave family. (I wasn't more than 8 years old.)

*Rod Swift*

Lingfield, The Old Prison and the Pond c1955 L50009

## Falling in the pond

*Rod Swift remarked about people falling in the pond - well I was one of these. Rod must be my cousin's son, as my aunt and uncle lived in the house referred to. Around 1953 on an icy cold day in winter, a crowd of us were going home after school. On passing the pond we knew there was thick ice so we decided to skate on the ice. We did not take into account that it was beginning to thaw and around the outside you could see the ice had melted. Quite a number of us went on the ice and most were fine, but I was in the rear and suddenly the ice caved in. I don't remember how many were actually in the water but I was very lucky as a bus inspector waded in and pulled me out from under the ice. Fortunately no-one was injured, and I only had hurt pride as my mother made me undress outside in the cold. I wish we could have thanked the bus inspector, but we never knew who he was. With regard to the old oak tree that can be seen behind the old prison in the background of this photo, I remember many a time standing inside the trunk, and we used to throw knives (holding the blade) to stick in the trunk. Nobody ever came to harm with knives in those days. We were always climbing trees and playing in the fields, making dens anywhere there was cover. We played with fag cards and marbles and five stones ('chucks' they were called where my mother came from in the north-east, and where we spent most of the summer holidays). My sister was fortunate not to be killed by the bomb that landed on Lingfield Primary School on February 9th 1943 during the Second World War. A few minutes later and the school would have been filled with 280 children and their teachers. Two teachers and two 11-year-old girls plus a caretaker were killed which included Mrs Lumsden, a teacher, and the wife of Mr Lumsden, one of my school teachers. I guess our whole family was lucky as an unexploded bomb was found at the bottom of what was our garden only in 2002 when builders were digging foundations for an extension to a house. It is said that the bombs were for the Monotype factory which was a munitions factory at that time. My cousin and I used to shop for our grandparents who lived in Plaistow Street, facing the prison which we called the 'Old Cage'. The house can be seen in one of the photos of Lingfield on the Frith website. Grandma used to send us to the local garage to get the accumulator recharged for the radio. We had to be very careful as it was acid. At Christmas all aunts, uncles and cousins visited here for a good old sing-song, while Granddad played the accordion.*

Jean Chambers

*'If you hadn't fallen in the pond, you were not from Lingfield!'*

## The Village I Knew

I used to live at Raymead which was a complex of 24 prefabs, they have been replaced now by a new estate. I come back to Lingfield every year to see the village I grew up in. When I got married to a local lad in 1963 we moved to Tandridge, unfortunately it didn't last due to me but we used to walk to the village pond at night and there was one night at Christmas when it was snowing and they had put fairy lights round the tree by the prison, it looked so lovely I will always remember it as long as I live. I lived there from 1942 - 1965. *Lydia Peyton*

## The Old Cottage

This cottage was in Bedford Lane in Frimley Green. I lived in a house called Connemara, which still stands in Bedford Lane. My father, Samuel Richardson, and his brother George were bricklayers. They had the job of demolishing this cottage and they were burning the thatch. My brother John was playing dare. He walked through the outer edge of the white ash of the fire and dared me to walk through the middle. Unfortunately I did, and was very badly burned. Mother rushed round all the houses, collecting tealeaves to put on my legs. (In those days people didn't empty their pots after every brew – they just topped them up with a little more tea and hot water.) I still do not know where Mother got the idea of the tealeaves. It certainly worked. I was left with just a few little scars, and they are hard to find. After demolishing the cottage, Father and Uncle George built a pair of red brick houses. A Mr Fairminer lived in the first of the pair, and I went to school in Frimley Green with his son.

*Mr D F Richardson*

## Blast From The Past

*Wow, did that ever shake me to the core. The names Richardson and Fairminer, Long and a few others sprang to mind as fellow pupils at the local Primary School. In those days I lived in Worsley Road. I can remember fishing the Basingstoke canal at Frimley Green and seeing the last barge go by which I believe was scuttled just before the flight of locks.*

John Oxford

## My Grandparents' Home

I received information from my cousin Leslie about this photo. Now that I have found it I am delighted. My grandparents were Thomas Benjamin Fairminer (1881-1954) who married Louisa Florence Smith (1880 - 1944). They raised 11 children, some of them at Bedford Lane. Their birth dates range from 1900 to 1924. My mother Florence Louisa (known as Ciss) was born in 1905. I remember visiting Bedford Lane as a very

Frimley Green, An Old Cottage 1906 54907p

young child, one of my mother's brothers, Alfred, lived a couple of houses down. A Mr D F Richardson shared information about this photo on the Frith website in April 2006. He says that he went to school with one of Mr Fairminer's sons, who must have been one of my uncles. I wonder which one it was? I am researching my mother's family and I have been able to get in touch with a number of cousins, many of them and their families still live in Frimley Green and in areas close by. *Joyce Hunt, Queensland, Australia*

## The Golden Farmer

I used to live in Maultway North - the turning directly to the right of the Jolly Farmer - in the mid 1980s, so I have hazy memories of the pub as a customer. But I remember feeling the place to be cut off from the rest of the world - it was always a challenge crossing the London Road as the pub is smack bang in the middle of a busy roundabout, a million miles away from this tranquil image. The legend of the Golden Farmer (where the pub gets its name) always fascinated me - he was a farmer by day but a highwayman by night who robbed rich travellers on their way to London. Famed for paying all his debts in gold, he was eventually caught and hung from the gibbet which stands near the pub, where he was left for all to see. His gold was never recovered and is rumoured to be buried nearby. My efforts towards finding the treasure remain unrewarded! No longer a pub, The Jolly Farmer was first transformed into 'The Mongolian Barbeque', a restaurant. It is now a golf shop.

*Julian Hight*

Camberley, The Jolly Farmer 1906 57182p

Dorking, Boxhill, The Wimpy Bar c1965 D45205

## My Weekend Job

*WOW, I never thought that I would see this postcard again. Yes, that's me doing my weekend job as a waitress at the funky new Wimpy bar on Boxhill. My name was Vanessa Howard and I lived at Ismanola, Boxhill Road. This was reputed to be one of the first Wimpey Bars in the UK, and locals, mods and rockers, and day trippers flocked to buy their Wimpy and Chips and Coffee, Knickerbocker Glory, Pepsi Cola in a glass bottle and all else Wimpy by the thousands. Hot doughnuts were a speciality with queues of folk waiting anxiously for their fix at 4d each or 4 for 1/-. Folk marvelled at the huge picture window which overlooked Dorking. Astute locals would return the glass Pepsi bottles to get the 3d deposit - it was quite a lucrative way of earning a bit of pocket money. Oh - and the washing up on a Bank Holiday was never ending! Situated opposite Upper Farm, the Wimpy bar was previously a tea garden and now is a restaurant.*

Vanessa Burgess

'Locals, mods and rockers, and day trippers flocked to buy their Wimpy and Chips'

# Down yer 'Wey'.

I moved to Farncombe in 1942 from Datchet, but was originally evacuated there during the Second World War from Barking, London. I remember arriving at my new home at 1 Tudor Circle. My step-father was a fireman in the AFS, whose own father, George Elliott, was employed as a shepherd watching sheep in the top fields on the left before Binscombe. Shepherds in those days were well looked after by the farmer, as a good shepherd could save many a lamb at lambing time. George used to bring home a rabbit or two during the war as he was well practised with a catapault, having much time on his hands when sheep watching. I remember 'Pop' Gibson, the Headmaster at the junior school, who would award a 'George' medal for reciting a poem from memory - the medal being a copper coin penny! He would have us do PT in the playground in the middle of winter, snow on the ground, stripped to the waist, all the time shouting 'Knees up! knees up' while I hummed the tune 'Knees up Muvver Brown'. 'Gibbo' wore a big black overcoat down past his knees, and a scarf and leather gloves. I remember he would shout out 'Stop, even if a bomb drops you will stay perfectly still'. We went swimming in the River Wey at the Colonel Grounds at the age of seven with bigger boys guiding us along across the river whilst doing the 'dog paddle'. Later we could dive in from the opposite bank and assist the bigger boys with 'pay back time', holding on the sides and rocking the day trippers' rented canoes, rowing boats and punts from Leroy's boathouse. One day a Spitfire crashed on the Colonel Grounds and we watched the pilot come down by parachute over Bunkers' Hill in the far distance. This gave us the opportunity to clamber all over the broken plane looking for souvenirs. Pieces of the perspex cockpit were favourite as we could carve out finger rings for sale to other kids. I had my first experience of competition fishing at Broadwater Lake, having joined the angling club as a junior, and my step-father, Jesse James Elliott, put tacks along a bamboo cane I had just chanced to come by from Broadwater Lake, a converted Yo-Yo acted as a reel and held a long piece of strong twine, a chicken feather, lead shot and a hook completed my equipment. Oh, and a ball of bread dough. On the day, having been allocated a position next to a real fisherman, he told me that I couldn't take part without having a keep-net plus a landing net. I thought this was a bit cheeky of him, so in my best cockney voice I said 'Fanks a lot Mister, but yer see I've been fishin' all mi life, so I knows jus what to do'. To cut a long story short, he set me up with his spare equipment and at the end of the competition couldn't stop laughing at the weigh in, when I won a new bakelite reel for second place for having the best basket of small fish, roach, dace and gudgeon. What a life! We used to go to the Guildford Lido and the indoor baths at Castle Street, although we didn't like the indoor baths so much as the attendant would shout at you for making too much noise and order you out of the pool, anyway it always had far too much chlorine and that would get up your nose and make you sneeze a lot. The Lido was our favourite - 6d to get in and putting your clothes in a steel locker. Having a fibre disk on a piece of string round your wrist with your locker number, you could then take your sandwiches and bottle of Tizer and spend all day swimming or sunbathing on the grass behind the fountain. I remember the girls, especially at the junior school - Dawn Elliott and Valerie Greenwood were my favourites. I remember my first paper round at Farncombe; six shillings seemed like a fortune in those days

Godalming, Old Boarden Bridge 1906 57056

when I could buy three comics - Champion, Wizard and Hotspur all 3d each, a couple of bullseyes or a bag of blackjacks and the rest of the money was handed to my mum. Mind you, one of the kids at school, a little on the plump side, used to get teased and bullied a lot, so he gave me a tanner a week to protect him. No trouble there, because I was friends with the bullies. Mind you there were those older boys who would bash me up because they said I was a foreigner from London. Of course we loved the barber down the end of St Johns Street - boys only on a Saturday morning. He spoke in what was referred to as pidgeon or clipped English - he may have been Italian? He used to say 'You lika da new airstyle, Sir, wiv nice spray afterwards?' A long white taper would be lit up and flicked up the back of your hair. 'It stop's the 'air from fast growing', he would say. The other boys sitting waiting would whistle, taking the 'mickey', but then with a big flourish the sheet came off and he would hold out his hand for the sixpence whilst helping you on with your jacket, brushing you off with a big paint brush and saying 'See you soon, Sir'. Walking back down the road with a swagger, whistling, you felt like a film star, imagining that all the girls passing by were admiring you or your haircut.

*Arthur Bird*

Virginia Water, Holloway Sanatorium c1955 V4028

## Nurse Hampton

Virginia Water, Holloway Sanatorium. On August 13, 1961 I took up residence as a student nurse in Lindsay Smith House across from the hospital. It was the day the Berlin wall went up, and, as I recall, the day before the grouse shooting season began. I was 19 years old. Miss Goodyear was the Matron. Miss Lemon was Assistant Matron; Miss Mitzi Tauber was Assistant Matron (rumoured to be the cousin of Richard Tauber the singer); Miss Cottingham was Night Sister. I wore a blue cotton dress, a white apron (fresh daily), a plain cap, black stockings and shoes. I was also issued a navy blue cape with a red lining. It was so cold dressed thusly, I made a red flannel petticoat and combinations to keep warm. We were not allowed to wear a cardigan, unless by special dispensation, like when the boiler was not working. We worked 12-hour shifts from 7am to 7pm for four days. One day, we were on at 10 am. On our days off we were served breakfast in bed by Italian maids. The trays had a full complement of food, hot cereal, tea, and little jugs containing milk. We spent three months, on probation, took a state exam after one year, and as part of the four-year course, transferred to general nursing at St Mary's Hospital in Paddington. The qualification of Registered Mental

Nurse required three years at Holloway. I have so many memories. Turning our cloaks inside out at Christmas time so the red showed. Carrying lanterns to the staff houses to sing carols, ending up at the Lodge, the home of the administrator. I don't recall his name, but others are etched in my memory, and I will recount them later. When sitting with a patient one did not have to stand up to greet Matron. Otherwise, if one saw Matron enter, one went to Sister and let her know Matron was there to do 'rounds'. One approached any senior nurse with one's hands behind one's back! In the summer we went to the swimming pool down the street. We hung out at St Ann's Club across the street. We could dance and drink and socialize there. In season we would take patients to pick blackberries, then return to the ward (Dorothea Dix) and make blackberry pies. I was 'sister' on Jane Holloway my first year there, looking after twenty moderately senile dementia women. I gave medications, served meals, bathed them and wrote reports. One evening I was assigned to take patients to see the play, 'Orange Island', in a theatre in Windsor. One of the men was on Antabuse, a drug to counter alcoholism, and which makes a person feel very ill if he/she drinks. He went to the bar and indulged. I had to get a taxi to take him back to Holloway. Later, he apologized and presented me with a bouquet of flowers! The stage in the ballroom was the scene for 'Psychodramas', scenarios portraying patients with schizophrenia, manic-depressive, senile dementia, and how staff, put on the spot, would deal with them. These were inter-hospital events. Instead of teacher, or instructors, we had tutors. I recall Mr Armstrong. The gate on his house read 'Hobbit'. The hospital had an operating theatre, not used in 1961. I had a verucca removed from my foot in there. I also witnessed an autopsy of a patient I had known from the geriatric ward, Florence Nightingale. There was also a morgue where we transported patients who had expired. I remember one 'dark and stormy night', transporting a deceased patient out to the morgue with Miss Cottingham. It was quite Gothic! The laundry room, as well as the boiler room, was along an underground corridor about a quarter of a mile from the main building. On each side, locked rooms displayed antique furniture, presumably left by departing patients. There were some antiques still in use. I particularly remember a charming little heart-shaped table outside the library. A movie theatre was situated next to Clouston, the locked ward. The maids lived on the top floor in the tower. Most of them were from Spain. After a year, I was allowed to 'live out', and moved to Trumps Mill Cottage, Trumps Mill Lane, across from the Mickelsen estate. I shared half the building with a wall between us, with the gardener for the estate, Pat and Betty, and assorted children. I lived there when Pat came and told me President Kennedy had been shot. In the village of Wentworth was a restaurant called 'The Hawk's Nest', run by Jeremy Hawk. I think he was a movie actor. I have vivid memories of patients, and for obvious reasons cannot name them but they included the lady who had rescued people by helicopter, flying over France. The well-known writer's sister. The maid on Florence Nightingale, Mary, a then-called idiot-savant. I took her to my room in Lindsay Smith House and played a 78 for her, and the next day she played it perfectly on the piano on the ward. Willie who audaciously called everyone by their first name. We were formally addressed by the title, as in Nurse Hampton. Even Matron called us 'Nurse'.

*Patricia Hampton, SRN*

# The Doodlebug

When I was born in 1939 we lived at 97 Shelvers Way, but my very first memory happened in 1944 during the war. It was a lovely sunny day and my mother, Doris Parker, was going to feed the chickens at the bottom of the garden. I was playing outside when mother called out to tell me to go inside and into the shelter as there was a 'funny' thing in the sky. I never did get to the shelter, only the dining-room and the next thing I remember was a great bang, glass flying everywhere and a crystal fruit bowl on the sideboard exploding. A doodlebug (flying bomb) had landed in the field opposite our house causing quite a lot of damage. Soon a WVS (Women's Voluntary Service) van arrived to help, mainly, I think, by dispensing cups of tea but what I remember most of all is our neighbour, Mrs Everington, giving me a sugar lump, something I'd never even seen before!

*Ann Chapple*

Tadworth, Shelvers Way c1955 T1016

Claygate, The Parade 1952 C319018

## The Parade in the 1950s

*I lived in a flat over 12 The Parade (then a Garden Shop) until I was ten years old, from 1944-1954. Our gate was on the alley round the back. At the Hare Lane end of the alley were hung 'pig bags' - sacks where people put scraps to feed pigs (post-war, so still on rationing!). The other end of the alley went through to one of the brickyards that were then still around Claygate. A rag-and-bone man came along The Parade every week, perched on a horse-drawn shallow cart; we called him the 'Yak-Yoh man' because that was what his 'ragandbone' cry sounded like.*

Pat Verral

We called him the 'Yak-Yoh man' because that was what his 'ragandbone' cry sounded like.

# Mytchett Post Office

My family moved to the post office in Mytchett Road in 1956 when I was six. I used to catch the bus at the bus stop opposite to go to Ash Vale Primary School. Yes, on my own, clutching my penny ha'penny bus fare and reciting in my head 'Half to Ash Vale please'. I came home for lunch on the bus too. As I got older my friend and I would save the fare by walking home and spend the money in Mr Hudson's fish and chip shop - he also sold cheap sweets. Next door was a hardware shop (Eades) and a bit further towards the Miners Arms and Frimley Green there was a big white building that was a cafe. We used to run along there to get ice cream sometimes. Opposite was Rorkes Drift, a gravel road where I learned to ride my first bike. A large overspill council estate for bombed out Londoners was built up here but I remember a large disused garden, with lovely fruit bushes and trees and pigsties where we used to play out of sight of adults. Opposite the post office there was Mansells the newsagent and some other shops. On the other side of the post office garden was a little lane called, I think, the Potteries, or something to do with potteries, and it was a short-cut through to Coleford Bridge Road. My parents sold the bit of garden next to the lane as a building plot and retired from the post office in 1959 and we moved to 33 Coleford Bridge Road. I played a lot in the woods around the canal and lake and we used to paddle in the canal in the hot weather but it was dangerous as it was full of rubbish. When we first moved there you could hire a rowing boat or punt in Ash Vale to take on the canal. Great fun! The recreation ground was in Hamesmoor Road and when a prisoner escaped from Broadmoor Prison they would sound an old all-clear siren from there to let residents know. There were great facilities at the Recreation Ground. Toilets, a bowling green, putting green and children's play equipment. Once I was at a Sunday School party in the village hall and they wouldn't let us go home until someone from home collected us because there was a Broadmoor prisoner on the run. Other entertainment was on the ranges. The red flag flew when firing was taking place but we sometimes crawled to the spot behind the big targets even when the soldiers were practising and kept our heads down. We also collected mortar bombs. I remember telling other children that I knew which ones were exploded and which were not, but goodness knows whether I did! A regular sight was all the troop lorries coming through the village, with young soldiers shouting suggestive remarks at us girls. Farnborough Air Show, which was annual then, affected us quite badly. I was terrified of the loud jets - Fairey Deltas - and they had coloured exhaust in red and blue which used to stain the washing if it was left on the line. I think my mum got some compensation for ruined laundry once and I know my dad got compensated for broken glass in his greenhouse as they broke more than the sound barrier. Lots of the children at Ash Vale school had army fathers and my friend lived in Keogh Close, married officers' quarters. I found it fascinating to go with her to the NAAFI shop and round their base. Her mother was German and had a miserable time in England in that decade after the war. One of the boys in my class was Danny

Mytchett c1950 M300001

Schultz. He lived in a council house next to the school. We were told to be nice to Danny because he had had to leave his home, his father was a refugee. I know he missed school once because he had no trousers to wear that day, and he only had the poorest of worn-out plimsolls at the best of times. His family were probably the poorest. I had some lovely teachers at the school, but for one year, when I was about 8, I had a teacher called Mrs Munday. She was very fierce and used to give us a spelling test every Friday. Every word spelt wrongly would mean one rap across the knuckles with a ruler. I was a good speller but sometimes got the ruler. I felt very sorry for the children who could not spell and might get half a dozen whacks. Really bad behaviour got the cane. I had the cane a few times for talking in class. My happiest year was with Mr Hill in 'top class'.

*Faith Moulin*

# How I gave up smoking - in one day!

I was born in 1934 at Weybridge in Surrey, close to where the River Wey joins the Thames, thus offering the dual attraction of open countryside and water - a totally irresistible combination to young boys set free from the heavy-handed restraining influence of fathers by the advent of the Second World War! For a few miles before joining the Thames, the Wey comprised the original Wey Navigation, used for transporting barge loads of heavy goods via the Thames to London. Timber, coal, corn, flour, wood and even gunpowder were regularly moved up and down the waterway in the 16th and 17th centuries and during the war the canal was still in regular commercial use. The huge barges were pulled along the tow path by equally huge horses. We lads grew to love these gentle giants with their soft kind eyes and placid nature and we knew them all by name. They were stabled overnight in a large barn at Edwards Lock, where we helped to brush them down, clean the horse brasses and feed them apples 'scrumped' from a nearby orchard. We also collected the manure which we sold to neighbours for their gardens or allotments. As a special treat we were allowed to ride on the horses' broad backs for the final mile or so then assist with raising

Weybridge, View from Lincoln Arms Hotel 1890 23589

the sluices, thus filling the lock and allowing the gates to be opened, thereby enabling the barge to be lowered to the level of the Thames. Sometimes we rode out on our bicycles to Addlestone Lock to meet the barges, then hitched a ride back, having first loaded our bicycles aboard. I knew every inch of the canal, sitting atop the barge and spotting the secret places where moorhens and dabchicks nurtured their young and tutored them in the art of survival, where kingfishers flashed low over the water, demonstrating flying skills which no Spitfire pilot could hope to match, while sand martins busied themselves patrolling their nest holes in the sand bank. The vantage point above the water provided intimate views of water voles and rats going about their daily business plus numerous water fowl and a host of wild birds all of which I could recognise and name having been schooled by the bargees and their wives, who accompanied them on their journeys. Each barge had a tiny cabin at the rear where the bargees slept and ate, washed and relaxed before joining a flotilla of half a dozen or so other barges, to complete the journey to London down the Thames, pulled by a tugboat. These cabins contained a tiny coal-fired stove which provided for cooking as well as maintaining a constantly simmering kettle to supply endless cups of very black tea or sickly coffee. We were allowed into the cabin when it rained or, in my case, to dry off when I fell into the river - a not infrequent occurrence but fortunately for me my mother, being a champion schoolgirl swimmer, had instructed me in the art at an early age. In summer or winter these cabins were always oppressively hot yet the bargees' wives spent their days toiling away under almost intolerable conditions, cooking, sewing washing and ironing - or drying off odious kids who had fallen overboard! They all smoked clay pipes filled with 'shag' which resembled dehydrated dog turd until rolled between the palms and expanded into an apology for tobacco! Their blackened and broken teeth bore witness to years spent puffing away at this vile mess - goodness knows what it did to their lungs! One day an elderly 'bargess' offered me her pipe – 'Here lad - fancy a draw?' she said, as I waited huddled in a blanket sipping a cup of tar-like tea waiting for my clothes to dry on the clothes line over the stove. 'Warm your cockles - can't have you catching a chill now, can we?'. I took the pipe and tried a tentative puff. 'No, no lad', she said, 'Take a long draw - get it right down'. I obeyed and almost choked. 'Take it long an' steady - enjoy yourself', she said. I tried again - and again. Then I felt myself turn green on the inside. My stomach demanded to be let out and I barely made it to the side of the barge! I was convinced that everything I'd eaten during the past month was returning to the real world and I was about to pass on to the next! Men with sledge hammers were pounding away inside my brain and my legs had turned into blancmange. I gratefully sought refuge on one of the bunks whist waiting for my clothes to finish drying by which time we had reached the lock and tied up for the night. Pushing my bike home - I felt too unsteady to risk riding it - I resolved there and then that smoking was not for me, not ever! Footnote: The Wey Navigation, unlike many other less efficient waterways, survived the railway era and under private ownership continued to trade until well after the Second World War. The last owners, Stevens & Sons, donated the canal to the National Trust in 1964 and today it is one of the few financially self-supporting waterways, having no call on the Trust's general finances or on public funds. See their website for further information.

*Stephen Squires*

# Small boys' toys and other pastimes. A memory of Smallfield in the 1930s

A large number of our toys were made from wood, dependant on what tools were available in my fathers' shed, if it was unlocked! The only tools needed were a saw, a hammer and some nails. There were two basic things a home made wooden toy was required to do: (1) Be able to be pulled along by a string, provided it had wheels; (2) To float in a pond or stream. The shape was unimportant, imagination made it realistic.

Our play area was usually the road surface itself, footpaths for pedestrians were only just becoming necessary, car movements were reasonably slow which gave plenty of time to move out of the way. Few footpaths meant more ditches with running water so floating boats along them was popular. A boat consisted of any shaped object that would float from the smallest twig to a chunky piece of wood; penknives were popular in order to shape the wood so that the front at least was the correct shape.

Cowboys and Indians, Bow and Arrows and other adventure games were played in the woods

Occasionally there was a tunnel such as the one under the road at the corner by the existing garage and Chapel, a boat could get stuck under there so we went looking for it all the way through to the other end. Provided we could see an exit to daylight it was a popular pastime just going through it.

Cowboys and Indians, Bow and Arrows and other adventure games were played in the woods, upon which now stand Tudor Close and The Woodlands, in later years during the Second World War when the area was filled with soldiers it was a popular place to spot a courting couple. Some dared to include the soldier as part of their adventure, provided they could run fast!

Dinky Toys were the popular toy along with Hornby Trains, I don't recall any toys in local shops except coupon offers in breakfast cereals. Cornflakes or Wheat Flakes were called 'Force, fronted with a lively cartoon character called 'Sunny Jim'. We flew elastic band powered model aircraft named 'Frog'. We made paper aircraft shapes that flew. The only proper toy shop I recall was in Horley High Street, they stocked all the best toys.

Although we had toys, most of our time was spent outdoors; walking along a ditch or stream to look for the water source was a regular interest. Many boys collected birds' eggs, not me. I always followed the interest of making of things, Arthur Putt the blacksmith was a particular favourite to watch at his forge, for 6d he would make a hoop which we then rolled all the way home. As we grew older and bigger pram chassis were in demand, they had four good wheels and a firm cross support onto which we placed some form of boarding for a seat then either sat on it and pushed ourselves backwards or made someone else push us.

I lived in School Road at number 9. The nearest boy of my age was at the other end of the village in Plough Road, I would spend many hours with them as they had access to Kings Brickyard and all the wonders of a building site, in particular there was water in the old clay pits, it was full of fish with perfectly clear water, some areas were too deep to venture into but the clay shallows were perfect. In winter local men skated on it but it was very deep in places, I was banned there.

Catapaults were popular, they could be bought from shops ready-made and were made of aluminium, or you found a hedge where suitable forked branches were growing which you then removed and shaped to a size similar to the shop ones. Lengths of square elastic provided the power, two pieces each about 8 inches long with a leather pouch in between the ends for ammunition, pebbles. They could be very deadly for hitting targets such as the china dollies (insulators) on telegraph poles or sometimes street lights; we aimed at rabbits but were poor shots. There was a definite hazard in using catapaults for if they were not held or aimed correctly the elastic or the pebble would hit your thumb or hand as it was released causing pain and bruising.

Climbing trees was most boys' pastime; any likely looking tree anywhere just had to be climbed

Fishing was always a good pastime, a stick, with a piece of string, and a pin with a worm or maggot on the end and dropped into the open stream near the garage, there was always the chance of catching a stickleback or minnow, sometimes we would try the pond at the side of Rede Hall Road just up from the shops where a big fat newt might take the worm. None of those caught would be 'hooked' as they would take the worm by simply sucking at it. All those caught would be returned in the same place.

In 1936 a village fete was held in one of Warnett's fields just up from the shops on the right with various events and races. There was a decorated bicycle competition where I was dressed as Micky Mouse. The winner of this event was John Prevett from Copthorne, his cycle was dressed as a yacht with himself as a sailor and he won first prize, there is no doubt his entry was good but I was jealous. There was free lemonade and a greasy pole, on top of which was a large ham, not very hygienic perhaps.

Climbing trees was most boys' pastime; any likely looking tree anywhere just had to be climbed, not me.

During the summer months when tar on the roads was near melting point, bubbles formed which if stamped on went off pop, this was all very well until our shoes became sticky, we then had to find some dry dust and jump about in it. When going to the shops or school after it rained, counting patches of coloured oil on the road was one game to see who totalled the most each day. Girls played hop scotch, girls were silly.

*Bill Haylor*

# Saturdays in the cinema – a memory of Epsom in the 1940s

During the Second World War, as youngsters we would look forward to the Saturday morning matinee at the Odeon cinema (4th building on the left of photo). Entrance was thruppence (three pennies). With our pocket money we would splash out on a penny peashooter with a packet of peas. The matinee used to start with a sing-along followed by a cartoon, then two half-hour films, the last being a western serial.

One that I remember well ended with the good guy entering the cabin and then it exploded, next Saturday's serial showed the guy coming out of the back door just before the explosion.

Bad guys always wore the black hats, this was the time for the booing, the good guys wore white hats, this was the time for the cheering. The noise was so loud the cinema manager would come up on the stage to ask the kids to keep the noise down, I'm sure it could be heard half way down the High Street, now this was the time for the peashooters.

Years later in 1955, when I was posted to Epsom in the Metropolitan Police, the Saturday morning matinee was still operating, with the same cinema manager. If I happened to be on the beat in the High Street on a Saturday morning he would call to me, 'Constable, come and speak to these children'. Not on your life was I going to stand up on that stage.

*John Forder*

Epsom, High Street c1955 E37053

Fetcham, Ford on the River Mole 1928 80801

## Rickety Bridge, River Mole at Fetcham and the Splash.

*I remember the rickety bridge over the River Mole here, when I was very small my mother used to take me over it to eat sandwiches by the 'splash' and go for a paddle. The bridge was really scary with wobbly planks and I was afraid of falling through where the missing one was. When I was old enough to go on my own I learned to swim in the river, hanging on to the water weeds and kicking my feet until I was confident enough to let go and 'doggie paddle'. I am not sure why that part on the river is called the 'splash'. Some say it is because it was once a ford and the horses splashed across, and others say it is because a bomb dropped in the river which made a big splash. The water is deep over the bomb crater which is still there. Last summer I was 60 and swam over the bomb crater and it was still out of my depth so I don't know how deep it is. I got some strange looks but couldn't resist it. Someone threw a ball for a dog which landed nearby and the dog seemed to think I was competing in a race for its ball! The rickety bridge has been replaced by one that I think was carefully chosen to resemble the old one, but there are no wobbly or missing boards.*

Ruth Gorst

## Hairdressers Banstead High Street

I worked as a Saturday girl at the hairdressers opposite the church in Banstead High Street when I was 15 in 1969. It was called Nicolette then and I worked for Margaret and her mother Mrs Anscombe. Margaret was a lovely boss, she taught me many things. The salon seemed huge to me in those days, but on a recent visit I was surprised at how tiny it is now. When I worked there we had separate booths and at the front was basins. The curtain was pulled across once the customer was seated within. I recall one client who worked at the church would request a foot stool while under the dryer and would read her bible while waiting for her hair to dry. Miss Deacon (Deaky) was her stylist. The salon also had a barbers attached and Ian and Trevor were the two barbers. Famous clients were Peter Osgood and Peter Bonetti - both footballers playing for Chelsea at the time. My school friends were really jealous of me over that! Ian was an amateur photographer, and I still have the photos he took of me, sadly I have no photos of the interior of the salon.

I used to 'Cardinal red' the hearth floor in the staff room and keep it spic and span. The towels were hauled up to dry on an old Victorian railed airer over a heater. I worked with Joan Townsend who lived in the village, she used to wash the hair and take care of the clients - and us. Elsie Henderson was the receptionist, I think she lived in Chipstead. They were both lovely ladies. The salon was taken over by Pam and Graham Attwell, in about 1971, by then I was an apprentice and was soon working for Margaret, a very talented stylist, we still keep in touch by Christmas cards each year. Teri and Mike Rabin took the shop over just after I left, they renamed it Oscar's after Mike's grandfather, the famous band leader - Oscar Rabin.

I can recall the camera shop, I think it was owned by Mr and Mrs Dexter, Mrs Dexter was a client, and the bakery, where we bought lunch - small shepherd's pies and Rum Babas! Woolworth's was across the road, it had the wooden flooring when I shopped there. I still have the metal back comb I bought there for 6p. I made my own clothes in those days and bought fabric every Saturday from a little shop by the bus stop, opposite Waitrose, near the roundabaout. One of my favourite clients was Mrs Bevan, she made marmalade for the village fete each year, she was in her 80s then. Nearly everyone had their hair set on rollers and I used to have clients come to me for half price while I was training. I charged 30p for a Shampoo & Set, rather than the full price of 60p! I had Marcel waving irons and learnt wig making (boardwork) at college. Pin curls were common and blow drying had just started to come into fashion. Nearly everyone had their hair permed and colouring was used to cover the grey rather than for fashion. How times have changed.

Banstead, High Street c1965 B391141

*Famous clients were Peter Osgood and Peter Bonetti - both footballers playing for Chelsea at the time.*

I have my own salon now - The Salon at Prestwood in Buckinghamshire, where I eventually settled. My mum still lives in Tadworth, so when I next go to Banstead I will take a recent picture of the High Street showing the salon as it is now. I have enjoyed looking at all the old postcards - well done Francis Frith, they are great.

*Karen Farrell*

## A Memory of Redhill swimming baths and town

Does anyone remember the old swimming baths at Redhill? I started swimming there in the 1970s when it was still a Victorian building. The steps in the pool were of stone and the changing rooms were around the poolsides with wooden doors. You could pay to have a slipper bath! There was a young lady who gave you a box to put your clothes in and you had to remember the number on it to get it back after your swim. Sometimes we saw cockroaches scuttling on the floor. I joined the swimming club 'The Marlins' and trained every Thursday with Mrs Ditzel. She seemed rather fierce at the time but she was just trying to get the best out of us. I also remember certain little shops along Station Road, a lovely old-fashioned chemist and a children's clothes shop called Hancock and Bean. There was a nice boutique near there which sold Mary Quant clothes which my mother used to love. I was really sad when Redhill changed so much in the 1980s. It seemed to lose so much character.

*Angela Middleton*

Redhill, Station Road East 1906 55033T

Caterham, The Barracks 1951 C49032

## Paper boy – A Memory from the 1950s

*As a 12-year-old I sold newspapers every morning outside the cookhouse where hundreds of National Servicemen were going through the horrors of their initial training in the Guards regiments. I believe they earned 28/6 per week, much of which they had to spend on boot polish, Brasso and Blanco! Their breakfasts looked pretty disgusting - porridge, greasy fried grub and then bromide-laced tea - all in the same mess tin. All the regiments had their own bands, so the sound of marching music echoed around Caterham on the Hill nearly every day. They had their mascots too - I really fancied owning the Irish Guards' wolfhound. Recruits used to go in, in their Teddy Boy drapes - and not emerge for eight weeks, by which time they would have been transformed into disciplined, clockwork men! After this preview of life in the Army, it's no wonder that 3 years later I joined the Royal Navy!*

Francis Younghusband

*Recruits used to go in, in their Teddy Boy drapes - and emerge transformed into disciplined, clockwork men!*

Weybridge, High Street c1955 W74049

## The Launderette

*I remember this picture very well. Just down the road from Woolworths by the white car, was a Launderette (maybe it's still there). This Launderette was the first one ever introduced to the UK from America in 1959. As we had no washing machine or dryer, this place certainly changed our lives. I can remember one day I was with my brother Bernard waiting for the washing and as usual went to look for some mischief (this time in Woolie's). On this particular day they were selling mousetraps for three pence each. Just for some fun we set each one (without cheese!) and watched with great amusement as customers picked them up and nearly had their fingers broken. Naturally we got caught and received a well deserved clip round the ear by the store manager.*

Dudley Piggott

This Launderette was the first one ever introduced to the UK from America in 1959.

## Mac May

I lived in a cottage by the pond some 25 odd years ago. My neighbour, well into her 90s, was Mac May (a version of her true name garbled by other neighbours' kids) who, every day, was out in her wellies digging in the garden. We had this photo and, knowing Mac May had lived in the cottage all her life, asked if she knew the children. She did and she remembered the photo being taken. The boy and the girl in the middle are Mac May's elder brother and sister; the little girl is Mac May herself and her brother has just thrown the milk jug at her (the small white object in the middle foreground of this view).

*James Moodie*

*The little girl is Mac May and her brother has just thrown the milk jug at her*

Ashtead, The Fish Pond 1904 52587P

# St John's Church in the 1950s and early 60s.

St John's Church has its own peculiar smell which I used to appreciate during 'the long kneel' (communion). Once a month (or every week), an army of children would be frogmarched from The Langsmead School to attend Sunday Worship. The Langsmead Room now is the only reminder of the now defunct Boarding School which the pupils funded by collecting a mile of threepenny bits. My friends and I went to Sunday School and thoroughly misbehaved ourselves but the vicar of the time was very patient with us. One day we were mucking around in 'the long kneel' when 'Goody Two Shoes Evelyn' reported us and dragged us off to see Mr Costin. We were petrified that he would find out we had been making my childminder's son turn head over heels in front of the altar and playing the organ without permission. He was, however, extremely kind to us and put our names in the birthday book. A few years later I belonged to the Children's Union and we used to do embroidery and sell our handiwork in aid of the Children's Society. One Friday, 22nd November, 1963, I looked at the clock whilst sewing a bib, and it was precisely at that moment that President Kennedy was assassinated by Lee Harvey Oswald in Dallas in America.

*Christine Beddows*

West Byfleet, St John's Church c1955 W456002

## Summer holidays

Wow! I was taught to swim in the Woking Pool by my mum. I could be in this very photo but preferred the quieter sessions. My sister or friends and I would cycle there and take a Thermos of Bovril to warm us up after our swim. There was a chalkboard at the turnstile entrance warning us of the water temperature! The changing room lockers were locked and unlocked by very sun-burnished attendants, and we had to poke part of our clothing (a belt, or sleeve of a blouse) through the door grille to identify our locker. Oh, the numb fingers and chattering teeth as we waited! Some people took their clothes to the poolside, risking getting them soaked by their mates! I loved the smell of the chlorine wafting across the park as we approached, and can almost hear the wind in those trees. The 'wedding cake' fountain was a great draw for those daring the wrath of the lifeguards. Although I had moved away by the time the pool was dismantled I was very sad to see it replaced by the ugly Pool in the Park.

*Frances Golynia*

Wow! I was taught to swim in the Woking Pool by my mum. I could be in this very photo .

Woking, The Swimming Pool c1965 W122050

# New Haw Childhood

*I have lived in New Haw most of my life. My family moved from Kings Road to Farleigh Road in 1949. One of my first memories was being taken to the New Haw Clinic for day care as my mother worked in London. There I encountered Nurse Lytle whom I met later at West Byfleet and Fullbrook School. We nicknamed her 'The Nit Nurse'. Pocket money in the 1950s was not very generous - but at the age of 5 I clutched 2d in my hand and made my way to 'Hunts' to buy either 4 blackjacks and 4 fruits salads (1d for 4) or a packet of polos. Mr Hunt first ran the shop solely as a sweet shop but later branched out selling wallpaper, paint and all things DIY - today the shop specialises in nail extensions and manicures. Next to him was the jeweller 'Mees' (which is now a hairdressers) - I used to do a lot of window shopping there. Kendals used to sell corn, chicken feed and hardware. The shop had a very peculiar smell - grain mixed in with turpentine. The floor of Brightwells butchers' shop was sprinkled with sawdust. Mr Cole used to run the fish and chip shop - and Mrs Cole always had a cigarette hanging out of her mouth and the nail varnish on her long finger nails was always chipped.*

*My friends and I used to play in the grounds of Woodham Lodge. In the 1950s and 60s the grounds had been terribly neglected and the house, which we called 'The Old Mansion', had fallen into disrepair. We thought it was haunted. It has since been demolished and in its place are new houses in Amis Avenue and the New Haw Day Centre. Summer holidays always seemed idyllic - we picnicked in Pyrford Woods or West Byfleet Recreation Ground, visited friends' houses and got up to no good, went on the obligatory Sunday School trip. It was not unknown to go on long walks or day-long bike rides. One of the highlights was visiting Woking Lido - not that we could swim very well but it was the 'coolest' place to be on a hot summer's day. Out on the street we used to play hopscotch, skipped, chanting rhymes, or had five-stones or jacks competitions.*

*Fullbrook School, Keston Avenue and the top half of Fullbrook Avenue were built when I was about 5. I started West Byfleet School in 1953 and my first teacher was Mrs Crab. It was not long after that The Grange School was opened. Because I lived on the West Byfleet side of Woodham Lane I still went to West Byfleet and at the age of 11 moved up to Fullbrook. The Geography Master, Mr Elvidge, cycled to school, pipe in mouth, wished you a good morning but would dismount and clip you round the ear if you failed to greet him. Mr Evans, the history teacher, had the most wonderful singing voice and at most end of term concerts would sing 'Blow me eyes, she did'.*

*I had an aversion to games and when we had to do long distance jogging, in the winter, my friends and I made a detour to my shed. There we brewed up tea and coffee because it was so bitterly cold. The kit, winter and summer alike, was thin cotton shorts and an even thinner top, short white socks and plimsolls. We all thought it was inhuman as the teachers were snugly wrapped up against the cold in warm coats or fleecy track suits. I can remember skating on the frozen Basingstoke Canal, sliding to school, throwing snowballs and making a catcher to collect all the frosted spiders' webs from the hedges.*

*The Old Library was part of All Saints' Church and has now been demolished along with two oak trees. In the 1960s the Youth Club met there but now we have a purpose-built 'den' built on-site.*

*New Haw Community Centre was extremely active. The Optimists used to put on a pantomime every year and it became a running joke that the Principal Girl always wore the same wedding dress and always married the same Principal Boy. The Dame, played by*

New Haw c1960 N183014

*Don Cobbam, who ran the Post Office for many years, always, always, always forgot his lines. One year, the villain, played by Charles Tozer, accidentally set light to the stage curtains - probably his most memorable performance. Gala Day used to be a sort of carnival day with floats and a May Queen but it did fizzle out, due to lack of support. For the past few years this event has been replaced by The Midsummer Event which takes place in Heathervale Park.*

*My friends and I were members of The Children's Union and used to meet in The Langsmead Room every Friday to do embroidery for 'the poor children'. We also belonged to Guides and The Red Cross and marched every year on Remembrance Sunday.*

*I left Farleigh Road in 1978 when I married at All Saints' Church with no view of the motorway bridge in site. Although some things have changed, some things have not, and I hope never will. New Haw still retains its villagey feel but Cross and Herberts, the Chemist, is now Lloyds and Turner, Garrett (without the Codgbrook) still are the Solicitors and Scotland Bridge has not fallen down - yet!*
Christine Beddows

## Saturday Nights in the 1960s

What memories this building holds. It gave the opportunity for a lot of teenagers to have their first Saturday night outs. It usually cost 1s 6d entrance fee unless there was a fairly well known group appearing that night then it was 2s 6d. I attended Redhill Tech (my surname then was Watts) and worked on a Saturday in Woolie's on the sweet counter and most of the day was spent chatting to various friends who used to come in and there would be great excitement in waiting for the evening to arrive.

I would rush home, wolf down some tea and then spend about 2 hours trying on outfits, usually wearing the first dress that I had put on. It was such an exciting time, minis were just coming in and there were clothes that were actually designed for teenagers and not trying to make them look like mini adults. One of my favourite dresses was a mustard coloured dress with black buttons and mock drop collars, oh I thought I was the bees' knees! I would meet up with friends and we would all troop off together (God knows what we looked like sometimes). We cottoned on to the fact that the groups would stay in the old South Eastern Hotel (does anyone remember that?) and I can vividly remember when the Hollies came to town and my mate, Liz and I just sat there looking and trying to sound cool when answering any of their questions. Liz came away with a chicken bone that night that Graham Nash had nibbled on. I wonder how many years she kept it.

And the handbags! A great pile on the floor, with all us girls dancing round while all the boys sat around the outside of the dance floor eyeing up the girls and trying to look big.

What groups did we have, well I remember the Hollies, Swinging Blue Jeans, Long John Baldry (I think, or is that wishful thinking?), Freddie and the Dreamers and lots more that have unfortunately slipped my poor old memory. They were such happy times!

*Sue Hoyland*

Redhill, Market Hall 1899 43148

Bagshot, The Church 1906 57176

## Clipping the hedge at St Annes – A memory from the 1950s

*My dad, Eric Berry, used to clip this hedge - BY HAND! When we're little, things always seem bigger than they really are, but my recollections of watching my Dad clip this hedge on the days he did the gardening at St Anne's Church were pretty accurate. It really is as big as I remember! I also recall going to St Anne's Hall (a bit further back down the hill?) with my mum, to collect our ration books. At the bottom of the hill was Fortuna's Ice Cream Parlour - I can still remember the luscious creamy taste! Yum!*

Liz Schultz (nee Berry)

My dad, Eric Berry, used to clip this hedge - BY HAND!

Ash, The Village 1905 53270

## Fond memories of Ash in the 1950s

*At the age of nine, I had to come and live with my mother's parents, Albert and Emily Warner, at 3 Church Path, one of a pair of cottages now pulled down, but their well - (what wonderfully tasting water, drawn up with a bucket!) still remains now in the front garden of the house occupying part of the site. The reason for my evacuation from Colgate, near Horsham, was that the flat we all lived in caught fire very early one morning and all we escaped with was one horseshoe-shaped door stop and our lives! The Warner's were a very green-fingered family. I recall big purple plums the size of a light bulb, raspberries, yellowberries, strawberries, very sweet apples, blackcurrants and gooseberries by the bucket load. Uncle Sid was a wizard with his chrysanthemums and other flowers, and their two big greenhouses (I can still picture their special aroma) were full of*

*tomatoes and lots of bedding plants. The Cannon pub (now converted to cottages) was the favourite Warner watering hole, and on the opposite side of the road was the King's Head (now also converted to private housing) where the 20c used to finish its journey and turn round for the return trip back to Aldershot. With these two ex pubs at each end of the base of a triangle, the building at the apex was a sweet shop and general store (this has also been replaced with private housing), I remember the lady owner who wore a full length black dress. I also remember being given some sweet coupons during the time of rationing, and joined a long queue to get my share. When it was my turn at the counter, I then found out that you needed some money as well to get the sweets! Just up from the Cannon pub (as was) was the real village blacksmith. The site of the forge can still be identified by the fencing arrangement by what is, or was, when I was last there, The Forge Garage. I can remember, with my head just above the bottom half of the stable door (top half open) seeing this man with massive forearms at work, and I can still recall the smell when he placed the hot shoes on the hooves of the horses. Next door to my grandparents lived a big middle-aged gentleman called Charlie Wheeler. Charlie, I now realize, had serious mental problems, and without any provocation or warning, would suddenly erupt into a loud shouting session, even when walking up Ash High Street. His mother, very rarely seen, was dressed literally as a witch, complete with pointed hat, and all in black. My grandparents' cottage did not have mains sewage, but had a cesspit sited outside the house at the end wall of the kitchen. Surprisingly this method did not produce any unpleasant smells, except when the lorry that emptied same arrived! Then you knew it! My granddad and Uncle Sid also had an allotment (they were a very self-sufficient family) in the area about 100 yards from their house, as the first corner turns to head up the hill to St Peter's Church (where my parents married in 1940, and where I also married in 1963). I also remember following this path through to Ash Common, where my Uncle Ted and Auntie Lil lived, and on this route was a bridge over the railway line, up near Winchester Road (still a notorious area, even then!), and it was great fun in the days of steam to stand on this bridge when an engine passed underneath. My Uncle Ted was a Signalman at Ash Station, when it was the box at the far end of the platform of the up-line (to Aldershot), and I recall helping him pull those big brass levers, and also having rides on the shunting engines that rearranged the trucks in the Goods sidings. Regular weekend trips were made in gangs of small boys to the nearby common land, passing the Dover Arms and up Ash Hill Road, and once in the ferns and pines, our imaginations ran riot. I remember long even temperature summers, never more than 70F, and cold winters where it never failed to snow at Christmas. Taking down of car numbers was, I remember, a good but not very busy hobby, as was the collecting of a wide range of cigarette packets. One good source of enjoyment was to record the originating depots of the British Road Services lorries that drove through, which were clearly marked along the side of the vehicle flatbed. I remember being given my first bike when I was about ten, and this was my Granddad's old 28" diameter wheel machine. I was always at the back of the racing group from the start, but once I had the bike rolling, I went by the others like a dose of salts!*

Ray Attwood

## A Nightingale Sang...

I well remember Banstead station in the 1950s. I used it to go to school in Wallington from 1953 to 1959 and then to go to College and then to work in London. At this time I lived in Nork and of course in those days the trains were all steam trains. My father used to go to work by train in the 1940s and always said that at 8.00am, standing on the platform waiting for the London Bridge train, you could hear a nightingale sing. Sadly as the station became busier, this ceased, but it was always one of his abiding memories of Banstead Station.

*Helen Perry*

*In those days the trains were all steam trains.*

Banstead, The Station c1965 B391114

Milford, The Roundabout 1935 86776A

## Royalty at Milford

*In 1962 I was in Cledwyn Evans's class at the primary school. In the summer terms Queen Elizabeth the Queen Mother used to visit King Edward's School in Witley, and Mr Evans led his class to the roundabout to see her go by. He was enthusiastically ragged about it by the other teachers! I remember on one occasion we all stood just by the walnut tree on the left of the picture. We waited, but not for long. The Rolls-Royce came whispering up to the roundabout and sailed past us. Then I saw the Queen Mum lean forward to tell her driver to pull up, and he reversed the car back to us. Mr Evans gulped, she waved and smiled at us through the window, then suddenly they were off towards Witley. I noticed Mr Evans was very red faced!*

Mike Taylor

The Rolls-Royce came whispering up to the roundabout and sailed past us.

## Early morning call

During the Second World War the pupils were evacuated and the school was turned into a temporary Maternity Home. The Doctor attending the home was only part-time, but always on call. The Doctor lived a few houses away and at night time he hung a length of string from a bell next to his bed and out of his bedroom window, so a nurse could run to his house to raise him if he was needed. Such was the case at 2:30am on the 10th of June 1942. I was born shortly thereafter.

*John E. Hutt, now living in Lewiston, NY, USA*

Ripley, Ripley Court School c1965 R36079

Bletchingley, The Village Butchers Shop c1935 B122005

## Selmes Butchers

*I remember being sent to Selmes the Butchers to buy my mother, Mrs Dora Maynard, cuts of meat. The floor was covered in sawdust and there was a little cashiers' office at the end of the counter. It always had a very friendly atmosphere although I used to cry when I saw the animals being unloaded from the lorries into the slaughteryard. Once or twice I saw them escape.*

Helen Swabey (Formerly Maynard)

## Saturday Jobs

My first job as a Saturday girl (1974) was working at a newsagents called Jarman's on the right of this photo on the corner of the road which led to the police station and infants school, Darley Dene. I remember having to weigh snuff and having to use an old-fashioned till where you had to add up the items and press down the correct keys to show the total in the top window. I worked for a lady called Molly - she was still there in the 1980s. I think I earned about 60p for a Saturday afternoon.

*Karen Rogers*

Addlestone c1950 A23023

# Buy my Lily of the Valley

On one day of the year, through the 1940s and probably the 1950s, my grandmother Ethel Glazier would pick all the lily of the valley she had, in a square bed about three foot square, in her back garden in Rowledge. She would bind them into small bunches, with leaves around, and tie them carefully with thread. They would sit in a bowl of water on the flagged floor of her larder overnight. She would be on the first bus from the village in the morning, and sit in the Castle Street end of this Colonnade, selling the bunches from a basket. She would be home in time for the midday meal, with a pocket full of cash, and a treat of fish heads for the cat (patriotically called Monty). My grandmother was a most respectable woman, and this was totally out of character, but I think she just liked to disprove my grandfather's maxim 'You can't eat flowers!'.

*Raela Croft*

Farnham, The Colonnade 1936 87793p

Weybridge, Queen's Road c1955 W74025

*She recognised her mother instantly from the distinctive hat, which she is also wearing in my mother's wedding photos!*

## My Grandma & Aunt

*Some years ago I gave my mother a book of Old Weybridge photos for Mothering Sunday as this is where she was brought up. Imagine her surprise, on seeing this picture of Queen's Road in Weybridge, to realise that the two people on the far right were her mother and younger sister, Edith and Lesley Johnson. She recognised her mother instantly from the distinctive hat, which she is also wearing in my mother's wedding photos!*

Gill Hicks

# Family Day Out - Clerkenwell to Caterham 1925

The photo opposite depicts Dorothy Connor (née Step) aged 10, with her late mother Elizabeth Step (aged 46) and her sister, Florence Step (aged 21) having alighted from the 159a bus which brought them from their home in Clerkenwell, London, pictured outside the Old Surrey Hounds Public House, Croydon Road, Caterham, Surrey on a day out to Caterham in 1925. They were on their way to the Barracks Hospital to see Dorothy's Uncle Charlie (her father's brother) who was in the army hospital. Wearing a pull-down bonnet and a typical twenties dropped-waist shift, the young Dorothy and her family had no idea they had been caught on camera. It was not until Dorothy was looking through a copy of Helen Livingstone's book about Surrey from The Francis Frith Collection some eighty years on that the exciting discovery was made. Dorothy said: 'My son, Dave, knows I like old books and pictures and as an early birthday present he bought me the 'Surrey Photographic Memories' book. I looked through it and was absolutely flabbergasted; I really couldn't believe my eyes. I showed the photo to my three nieces (Florence's children), who are now in their late seventies, and they were absolutely delighted. We have our own photos of Mum and Florence wearing the same outfits as they were in the Frith photo - it is amazing!' On Dorothy's 90th birthday, there was an article about her in all the local Surrey papers which showed her as she is today alongside the Frith 1925 photo. In fact, Dorothy has become somewhat of a local celebrity in Ashtead with fans in all the local shops. She is frequently recognised, following the newspaper articles and enjoys her newly-found celebrity status! Even the landlord of the Woodman Public House in Ashtead has hung the picture on the pub wall! The Old Surrey Hounds Pub has not changed its outward appearance much in all these years, and the landlord of the Landlord of The Old Surrey Hounds happily displays the Frith photo on the pub wall. The East Surrey Museum also has a copy of the photo in their archives as does the Surrey History Centre at Woking.

*Elisabeth Connor*

Caterham, Bus in Croydon Road 1925 78135t

Chipstead, Station Parade c1955 C484023

## Our childhood above the shop

We moved into this parade of shops in 1938. Our father opened a green grocery and florist shop at No 16 I think? Although the war years were devastating to many people, I recall many fond memories of growing up in Chipsted with my older sister Valerie. Our father was serving in the national fire brigade and managed to come home from time to time to help our mother run the shop and raise me and my new sister Elizabeth. During this period we were taken to Merthyr Tydfil in Wales along with many children. I also recall that one of the first V1 rockets crashed opposite the shops. All of us children ran over to look at the wreck and quickly got chased away by the Home Guard. Colin Grimes was one of our good friends, his father ran the grocery store which was the second from the top. We recall that during these hectic times we spent many hours in the Morris shelter that our father had installed in the basement. Many times we came upstairs to be greeted with windows that had been blown out by explosions nearby. Our mother had to frequently come and chase us back into the house because as children we wanted to watch the dog fights above us. On VE Day we, like many places, had a street party. Valerie remembers that Mrs Grimes made home-made ice cream especially for us. We all had a good time, but I recall that my mother was most upset that somebody walked off with a couple of her glasses. While trivial today, back then in 1945 one could not just run out and purchase new ones. It was after the war that our father bought the shop next door as an ironmongery and had the Post Office moved up from another shop down the parade. During this period our youngest brother Derek was born; we left in 1946 for Sussex and a new adventure in our lives.

*Brian Silk, Calgary, Canada*

## A happy childhood in Godstone, from 1950 onwards

I lived in Hillbrow Cottages on the Eastbourne Road from 1950 to the 1970s. My father, George Mison, worked in the sand quarry in Bletchingley and my mum, Elsie, was a housewife. There are only 12 cottages at Hillbrow and so there were about 7 children around the same age, David, Susan, Michael, Wendy, Ian, David and me. We used to play up on the common or paddle in Diana's Fountain. If you went further along you could swim in the river, where it wasn't unusual to see a snake or rat swim past. It used to be full of all the village children if it was hot. Sometimes we would take a sandwich and go up White Hill for the day. There was Hillbrow Guest House on the corner of Hickman's Close. You could go to the back door and buy ice lollies. They were lovely people, it was sad when it was knocked down and new houses were built. No one ever locked their doors and if anyone needed help it was always freely given.

My great-gran Matilda lived with us and she had a lovely garden at the front, you would see her out there weeding, and sometimes she would pull out a snake and throw it into the road (the A22). She said the cars would run it over but we only saw a few cars a day during the week.

We used to play up Bull Beggars Lane. I tried to learn to ride a bike there, my dad would take me to the top and let me go. I still have the scars today and still can't ride a bike! We would dig camps out of the sandy ground and race our go-carts down the lane and try to turn the corner without falling off. Through Love Lane and we were at what is now Godstone Farm. Mr Almond was the farm manager and we used to play there a lot. Now we would have to pay! We had a big old tortoise, Oswald, he lived on the front lawn in a little house, then Esmeralda, another big tortoise that had literally fallen off the back of a lorry going up Tilburstow Hill, was brought to live with us.

The Brooker brothers ran the village shop and I actually worked in there when it was owned by Finlays. The Barnard brothers delivered the coal. Mr Stacey delivered logs and Mr Dowling came once a week with a station wagon loaded with everything from dusters to candles and vinegar sold by the pint. Mum would send my brother, David, off to get a pint of vinegar and he would drink most of it before he got home.

We went to school at St Nicholas School at the top of Church Lane and walked up 'the bay', with the bay pond on one side and The Alders on the other. I remember running along the side of The Barn one day following a little path, slipped and rolled down through the stinging nettles. Ouch! Mr Harding was the Head Teacher, Miss Cannon was a teacher, I think she lived in Tandridge. There was also 'Dynamite', I can't remember what her real name was, Miss Howard maybe, but if you upset her she went off like dynamite.

At 11 we went off to St Catherine's Secondary in Bletchingley. Mr Shepherd who had been a teacher at Godstone switched over to St Catherine's. He was a nice man, he taught us to play stool ball. We used to play in Fairalls sand pit on the Eastbourne Road, looking for lizards. We never hurt them, just looked at them and released them. My best friend Ian Mcpheat and I went down there after we had had a lot of rain. Big mistake! We kept getting stuck in the gooey sand and losing our wellingtons. No one knew where we were and it seemed to take hours to get out. We finally managed to get out and a really kind lady in one of the houses in Eastbourne Road took us in and warmed us up. We got into a lot of trouble and I think our parents had called the police, so it was really serious. I was so glad that Ian didn't leave me.

Godstone, The Village Green c1955 G27030

Gran used to go to visit Mr Sparrow in North Park Lane to buy apples. She had a shopping trolley that my dad made for her, a little wooden box on wheels with a long curved handle to pull it with. She always had a little crochet bag with her. She was born in 1867, and wore her long white hair up in a bun, a black coat and dresses that went neck to ankle with long sleeves. Gran's daughter, Grace (Sadler), lived with Carol next to the undertakers in Needles Bank. It never bothered her but it was a bit creepy. She had gas lighting downstairs only and an outside toilet that was a long wooden seat over a hole. I never asked any details but it was great if you needed to use it! The Village Stores were wonderful. Mum worked there part time for a while. The brown sugar was weighed out into strong bags, in fact everything was weighed out. Upstairs was a treasure trove for me. I was allowed to go up there and wait for Mum. Cupboards, door and drawers all in brown wood, I'm not sure if it was stained or painted. I think the owner was Colin Hall.

There was a breakdown garage for cars at the top of the high street, Sparks, I think. I was given a cannon ball by the workmen that dug it up from outside the Bell around 1958, I still have it. Emily Catlin ran the St John's Ambulance Brigade, she was such a lovely lady. How she put up with us I will never know. I always think of Godstone as my home. Good memories.

*Ruth Bradbury, nee Mison*

## Changing Times

I was a Chiddingfold child. My father was from Milford (Cozens) and his mother and father owned the little newsagents/grocery shop on Manor Road. My mum was from Shackleford (Reffold) and I didn't move far away – Godalming – and some of my siblings still live in Chiddingfold today, my youngest brother in the family home with his family and pops. I remember the Laggs and taking my first swim in the brook, jumping off the bridge, going to the bottle dumps, even in the 1970s there was no H&S, we had the best childhood ever. We were in the woods at the back of Hartsgrove from 9 in the morning until late in the evening, we used to make camps, wooden jumps and had Whippey sticks for imaginary horses (my sisters and I often called our horse Glamour, after our Aunt Hilda's horse). I remember Mum calling us from the bottom of our garden for dinner. All the kids in Hartsgrove used to play in the woods – it belonged to the Moores from the farm and the grandson I believe still owns the woods but the farmhouse was pulled down and its site is now Woodberry Close. We used to cycle around Vann Lane into Hambledon and just take a bottle of squash and a jam sandwich, our parents didn't worry about us, we seemed to be safe. It is very sad but I wouldn't let my daughter do that now. Bonfire Night in Chiddingfold was always a big event, the roads were blocked off, you had to get back in the village by 5pm or you wouldn't get in. Mr Bull and Mr Young (the butchers) would provide this lovely pork, roasted on a spit. There was always a procession of lanterns and a talent competition in the old village hall (which now has houses on). My sisters and I entered one year as the girls from St Trinian's, we never came anywhere but it was fun. The fireworks were fantastic and we had people from miles come to the village, even the BBC. Then at Christmas we had a trip to a pantomime for the children via the members of Chiddingfold Ex-Servicemen's Club. Saturday nights there were bands on, this was a family event, our parents and their friends would take the kids out for a dance on a Saturday evening. They also had radio DJ's, wrestling, and auctions at the Club, and the famous band Genesis used to practise there. I remember Hills, the little bakers/grocers, the little RACS (Co-op) that used to be on Woodside Road before large superstores, and the local ladies that used to work there. I went to St Mary's School, and the fantastic lunches we had there! I remember waiting at afternoon break for the tray of left-over sponge jam and coconut pudding to be distributed (first come first served), that was a competition, getting some left-overs, they wouldn't dream of it today!! I

Chiddingfold, The Village c1955 C85005

remember being scared to walk down Woodside Road in the dark to go to Brownies and Guides, or the shops for Mum. There was a big laurel bush from the Matthew's garden and Shrimp's field on one side (Shrimp was a big white horse that belonged to the Harris family) and slopes of woods on the other. Both sides now have estates of houses on them. I even remember Sunday school at the Baptist church, which my stepfather's family attended several times a week (the Mitchells). Those are the fond memories and days of a Chiddingfold child – I hope there are others who remember those days!

*Nicola Cozens*

# An Evacuee Remembers

A South Londoner, I was 12-plus when the Second World War started in September 1939. I was evacuated with Wandsworth Central School to Farncombe in Surrey, and remember sitting on the floor in a large hall waiting for someone to 'adopt' me. Eventually, I found myself with the Gorringe family who were the local Builders, Decorators, Undertakers etc, in Hare Lane. I have nothing but very happy memories of my time with them which lasted until 1942, when I returned to my parents back in Wandsworth. This was to a new home, for the old one had been destroyed by bombs. I have nothing left of my childhood except memories and one book.

With the Gorringes, I was treated like the fourth son of the family – the junior of Bertram, Keith and Stanley, the three existing sons. In Farncombe, I saw apples growing on a tree, I went ice-skating on Broadwater Lake and tobogganing on Bunkers Hill, all firsts in my life. I have many memories of Eddy Leroy, the son of the then boathouse owner on the Wey at Catteshall (I think). Eddy ran the Sunday King's Own Bible Class, and used to take us on river trips in canoes and punts, and also on exciting games in Compton Caves which were nearby. I did my first and only paper round in Farncombe for WH Smith, which entailed delivering around the Charterhouse area. I also had to collect the weekly money, and remember getting into a first-class mess the first time I did it. Our schooling was almost non-existent to start with, but eventually we were housed in the Technical College in Meadrow, a year or two later moving across the road to an existing school. I was a useful footballer and cricketer, and played for my school at cricket against a Charterhouse eleven and can remember scoring twenty eight runs. I also played a few football matches for what was, I believe, Farncombe & Godalming FC. I probably played only because most of the usual players were militarily engaged. Mr Wright, who was something to do with the football club, was also the owner of the Chemists at the corner of Hare Lane and Fern Road, and I worked for him in the shop on a very part time basis. I can remember helping to make face powder, and serving in the shop. I experienced many happy visits to the County Cinema at the Meadrow end of Hare Lane, but I know this no longer exists. Hours were spent in the recreation ground in Lower Manor Road and I was very friendly with the man employed (presumably by the Council)to keep things tidy. I must have collected up tons of leaves. It was in this recreation ground that I saw some luscious apples on a tree, in the back garden of a house fronting Wolseley Road, and I promptly went scrumping, only to get caught by the occupants! The man was the local Rector, and as Mr Gorringe was a Church Warden, I was expecting to get into very hot water. In the end, I got a small reprimand, and never stole again.

Farncombe, Farncombe Street c1955 F10017x

I remember very few of the friends I made in Farncombe, but I do remember a couple of the girls – one was Lorna (surname unknown) who lived in The Circle, or The Oval, and the other was Eileen Sawyer who lived in More Road. I have been back to Farncombe on a couple of occasions, but it has changed so much that I was very disappointed. It is no longer the quiet village I knew, but is all hustle and bustle – presumably the result of the motor-car age. Sadly, all the Gorringes I knew have passed on, and I am grateful that I stayed in touch and was able to thank them for what they did for me. I do occasionally email a grand-daughter of Mr and Mrs Gorringe who lives in Canada. I would like to say thank you to Farncombe and its people, for giving me such happy memories and making me welcome when I was temporarily parted from my family.

*Ronald Waller*

## WH Newson

On the right of this photograph is Rushworth Road. When I joined WH Newson they occupied the land that is now the Canon office and Homebase. Newson's was a timber merchants with sheds full of timber, boards, fencing products etc. Customers would come in, see one of the staff who'd accompany them to the yard and start collecting their items. I'd just left Reigate Grammar and was living in Raglan Close with my parents. We used to drink at the Bulls Head in Reigate on a Friday/Saturday. Newson's was run by a larger than life chap whose name escapes me. Morris someone? Staff would occasionally go to his home to spend the day doing DIY or whatever. My manager there, Rick Beard, and I would stroll over to the railway sidings and hard-standing and race our radio-controlled cars on the redundant British Rail-owned area after work (sometimes during!). It was a large expanse of concrete, the remains of which are still visible if you go to the far end of the Homebase car park. You could walk all the way from there parallel to the train tracks, to the shabby shops fronting London Road. I remember a cafe there where we would have bacon butties on those cold winter mornings. In the photo below, it may have been one of those buildings on the right, maybe two or three up from Rushworth Road? The Newson's land was sold and next thing we knew it was a Texas Homecare and an office block. Then Texas became Homebase and here we are in 2012. You know what makes me most nostalgic – remembering standing outside the shop on London Road chatting, eating the butty, and not really noticing any traffic. Try pulling out of Rushworth Road now!

*Andrew Pennell*

Reigate, London Road c1965 R20240

Merstham, High Street c1955 M67017

## Olde Tyme Dances in the Village Hall

I remember the 'Olde Tyme' dances held in the Village Hall at Merstham once a month on a Saturday night in the 1950s. At seventeen you might think these would be too sedate for a teenager, but with my dad's old suit borrowed on the way out, and lively group of friends, dances like 'The Lancers' or a 'Quadrille' could be anything but sedate.

Although frowned on by our elders, eight youngsters going round in a tight circle with linked arms could have the female partners sailing well above the floor. The other dances were fine, with some being progressive, where you danced with every woman in the hall. So many of those fun people have unfortunately now gone, but are not forgotten. Sometimes the following week the Surrey Mirror would publish a photo of all who were present. I wonder if anyone else remembers dancing to the live band?

*Tony Tester*

# Smallfield Prepares for War 1939-45

One of the first indications in the village relating to the Second World War starting in 1939 was the erection of a telegraph pole, on the top of which was a platform and a circular metal object about the size of two buckets, called a siren; at each end was a circular slotted opening out of which came the creepy but familiar wailing sound. This siren was placed opposite the (old) school in School Road (Redehall Road) and just within the entrance to Gonville Laundry. During use the indication of an imminent air raid was a warbling sound, then when all danger had passed a single tone was sounded. During the war all church bells were silent, the sound that everyone most feared were the church bells ringing again for this would mean that England was being invaded.

During 1940, and to counter enemy movements across southern England, deep gullies were excavated and referred to as Tank Traps. Smallfield had its own section; they crossed Chapel Road running east to west at a point just above the row of bungalows and below the detached houses on the left. They were 10 feet deep with one side angled and the other vertical, supported by upright poles to prevent collapsing. They were expected to halt the passing of enemy tanks across open countryside. To make these deep angled cuts, earth scrapers were used. Over time, water settled in these deep gullies and the sides collapsed. As 12 year old children we watched all these preparations and then played in them when the soldiers had gone.

To accompany these gullies as they traversed the countryside, hexagonal gun emplacements built of brick and concrete were built and known as Pillboxes, there were around 5 in the Smallfield vicinity but they have mostly been demolished.

The Blackout was a scheme devised to prevent the enemy seeing any likely targets at night. Everyone was ordered to cover all windows to prevent light escaping; even the slightest chink would receive a knock on the door from the police. Lights on cars had to be fitted with special masks, making it impossible to see where you were going, so speeds were reduced to almost walking pace. Windows had to be decorated with sticky tape in a criss-cross fashion so that if they were broken by a bomb blast they would fall in small pieces and be less dangerous.

Air raid shelters became available in several forms, some were like a metal box that went under a table indoors, whilst others were of corrugated iron that stood outdoors. Many people made their own by digging into earth banking, where they would sleep at night; I can vouch that they were very comfortable and rather like camping. What our parents thought must have been grim.

As food became short Ration Books were issued, for there had to be some arrangement whereby everyone was treated equally, in reality it was a little different but we all survived. Village folk had an advantage over town people in that rabbits and pigeons could be shot or caught for meat, and many people were already well equipped for growing all manner of fruit and vegetables. Chickens and ducks were easy to rear for producing eggs, while tame rabbits became popular for the table, when they were skinned and ready for cooking they looked no different to wild ones and be assured they were very tasty!

Various schemes were devised for the protection of others, one being the organising of an Air Raid Warden whose duties would be to ensure that everyone obeyed government orders regarding safety and public order. The TV series 'Dad's Army' gives a fair indication of how a warden dressed and what he did. I have no knowledge who held that post in Smallfield.

There was a Home Guard group in Smallfield, I can recall one or two members who were very much like 'Dad's Army', mostly older men who were not required to join the army due to age or health. One of their meeting places was the Church Hall opposite Burstow Church.

One very important happening was the arrival of evacuees from London, some from Brockley, some from Mitcham. As has been described in other places over the years, there was a pecking order, or better described as a 'picking' order, by those who decided they were better qualified to 'choose their child' from the large number of unknown types that lined up that day in the school playground. Unwritten hierarchy in Smallfield dictated who chose which child, it was a matter of who had first pick, it was likened to a cattle market! The last child was of a different racial background, slightly coloured, the parent had assumed there might be a problem and had sewn a £5 note inside his clothing.

Of the people who decided to take in children, there were some who already had children so an extra one or two would mean little change, while other families I knew were childless but decided they would be patriotic and do the right thing. One childless lady near me in School Road took in three brothers, twins and a single from Brockley. It was hell, she told my mother, they had never used knives and forks to eat with before and when it came to using the toilet at night (there were no toilets indoors), a chamber pot was the usual container, which the boys were not used to, so they simply peed on the floor.

Unwritten hierarchy in Smallfield dictated who chose which child, it was a matter of who had first pick, it was likened to a cattle market!

Another boy I knew well was selected by a well-off family but he hated it, he never had enough to eat and eventually asked to be moved to another family where he stayed until returning home. In our house we had two boys from Mitcham, as far as I can recall we got on very well but I do remember getting jealous at one time when one appeared to be favoured more than me for food, but I suppose that's normal. The boys from Brockley also had a sister who stayed with us at one time.

*Bill Haylor*

# Early days in Mytchett

I was born at home in Coleford Bridge Road in 1935 and grew up there, went to school in Frimley and lived in Mytchett until emigrating to Australia in 1964. In those early days life seemed very simple, only a handful of cars, making street cricket safe. Everybody walked, our nearest shops were through the bridle path to the main Mytchett road, there we found Days Store, Dawes the butcher and on the other side of the road was Eades the shoe-mender and the Post Office, where I had a post office savings account as I grew up. Outside the shops was the bus stop for the Aldershot & District Traction Co (green) bus service between Aldershot & Woking and the yellow bus service between Guildford (I think) and Camberley. The nearest train station was Ash Vale, Southern Rail to London (Waterloo). I remember that the train arrival times coming back never tied up with the bus, so most times we had to walk home.

There were two farms in the road and behind our house was a large field where they grew wheat. I looked forward to harvest time with all the noise and bustle as the wheat was cut, the sheaves placed in stooks, in rows for the men to toss them on to the horse-drawn hay cart, using large and very dangerous looking pitch forks, before being threshed by the belt-driven threshing machine, powered by a great steam engine. At the end of the road was the River Blackwater, which in those days always seemed to flood with the winter rains, providing us kids with yet another adventure. The train line running alongside the river was the London South Eastern and Chatham Railway. Halfway along Coleford Bridge Road was 'The Copse', an area of woodland with a pond in the middle. Here we built our gang headquarters in the largest oak tree, dammed the small stream feeding the pond and caught newts using string with a worm tied on the end. The male or king newt was sure to get everyone's attention. Later on the same tree was used to spot fires breaking out in woods on the mostly army-owned land past the Basingstoke Canal and around Tunnel Hill. We would then try to find the fire area on our bikes – a dangerous business as there was a lot of unexploded ammunition lying around. I spent a lot of time fishing for roach from the banks of the canal, and there was a swimming hole along the canal towards Frimley Green, but our best swimming hole was on the far side of the lake where a sand bank extended out into the lake. Not a lot changed for us youngsters during the first part of the Second World War, but we could see the glow in the northern sky from the London blitz, and once or twice dived under the dining room table when we heard the 'Doodle Bug' engine cut out while passing overhead. There was lots of excitement one day when an escaped barrage balloon with its big ears floated over our house whilst being chased by a fighter. It was not brought down, probably due to the built-up area. We sometimes used to find black and silver foil lying around the garden and roads, which I believe was to do with aircraft radio or radar jamming. Toward the end of the war a German aircraft dropped a bomb, which made a large crater in a farm driveway along Mytchett Road. As I understand it, lots of people went to see it, and I heard tell the farmer charged a nominal fee for the privilege.

*David Greenland*

Pyrford, The School c1965 P338017

## Pyrford School in the 1960s

*My father was a teacher at Pyrford School when Len Cowie was the headmaster. I remember Mrs Jones and Mrs Bugler and Miss Mcdermot and Mr Stevens, who lived by the old school in Engliff Lane. I remember being privileged to sometimes miss class and go swimming in the pool when my dad was taking his class for a swimming lesson (he helped build the pool). Once when we were swimming the Beatles came on the radio with 'I Feel Fine', and I remember all the girls shooting out of the pool and running towards the radio (which was beside the pool), they ran screaming towards it! Days of simplicity, no mobiles and no computers! Did you know that in 1964 when building the infants' school they buried a metal box under the foundations and put in it the Beatles' record 'She Loves You' and newspapers from that day and other artifacts. To think that box is still there – I wonder when it will be un-earthed! Brilliant and very happy memories.*

Adrian Bray

*The Beatles came on the radio with 'I Feel Fine', and I remember all the girls shooting out of the pool and running towards the radio*

Shere, The Village 1903 50268

## Living in the Square at Shere

*I was born in July 1940 as Virginia Le Roux. The house on the left of the picture was where I lived until I was nearly 13 with my parents. The long narrow upstairs window was my bedroom. My mother's mother and brother also lived in the house. My uncle – John Grover – had a shop to the left of the porch, where he sold fresh fish, fruit and vegetables, some of which he grew himself. During the Second World War people would come from Dorking and Guildford to buy fresh fish. The fish came from Harlow's of Grimsby in wooden boxes; when the empty boxes were returned to Grimsby, my uncle used to fill them with rabbits and other game caught locally, because food was scarce due to food rationing. My uncle used to smoke kippers in a shed near the stream. He also kept the white ducks which swam along the stream. I have very happy memories of my childhood spent in Shere.*

Virginia Pawlyn

My uncle – John Grover – had a shop to the left of the porch, where he sold fresh fish, fruit and vegetables, some of which he grew himself.

# My grandparents, Mr and Mrs Denyer, the lock-keepers in the 1940s

I have very happy memories of my grandparents, who were the lock-keepers in the 1940s. My grandad had an enormous beard, and my grandma always wore a long flowered apron. At the back of my grandparents' cottage was a waterfall with a footbridge going over it, which lead to the outside toilet – there was no inside one in those days! Grandad used to sit me on the handle of the lock gate while he slowly opened it to let the water level rise or drop, so that the water level in the lock was the same as the river and then the barge could go on its way. My mother left New Haw to live in Grimsby, the only time I saw my grandparents then was when we came on holiday. As I got older the barge people would let me sail through the locks into the river and my grandma would get me off at the other side. I remember on one visit one of my little sisters had somehow got to the water's edge, nobody dared call her for fear of her falling in, it was a case of creeping up and grabbing her.

*Pamela Denyer*

New Haw, The Lock c1960 N183010

## The Teddy Boy Era of the early 1960s

I was born at the top of Reigate Hill (Mogador) and would catch the 406 bus every Saturday night to watch the latest films at the Majestic Cinema. We would visit most of the local pubs in the area such as the Market, the Bell, The Queens, and The Sultan (this was opposite the Co-op), and there was also the South Eastern, and the Locomotive – the Home Cottage we never used. My girlfriend's father was George Pearman who was the foreman at Kennings garage between the Locomotive and Surrey Mirror buildings, in Ladbrook Road. Some Saturday nights we would visit the old Market Hall in Redhill to watch a rock band, which most nights ended in a fight with the local lads from Merstham. The Ex-Servicemen's Club was in Reigate where I still drink on most Saturday nights and still call out the bingo. Our group of lads were called the Kingswood Cowboys, and our last port of call on Saturday nights would be the Market Hotel at Reigate for our last pint. We would watch out for the last bus (406) which would stop outside the White Hart, and would then run as fast as we could up Tunnel Road to catch the bus, however the driver and conductor would be laughing and waving to us as it sped past us which resulted in a long walk home, but not until after another drink at the Railway Hotel. When I started driving (my car was an Austin A35) we could drive up Tunnel Road, and the High Street was both ways. We purchased our records from 'Rhythms' in Church Street, and you could smell the home-made coffee from two doors up. Opposite the Tunnel bus stop was Wray Park Motors (which sold Rolls Royce cars) also in the parade of shops was a cafe, and behind them was Reigate swimming baths.

*Derek Chinery*

Reigate, High Street 1951 R20068

Guildford, The Roof Garden c1960 G65128

## Harvey's Roof Garden

*We moved to live in Hersham, Surrey, in the late 1950s and visited Guildford quite often through the 1960s. A visit to the Rooftop Café at Harvey's was always a highlight for me. I remember jumping from stepping stone to stepping stone, and watching the fish darting about in the water. I have never seen another rooftop café anywhere and I'm very glad to know this unique place is still in existence – I have very happy memories of it.*

Linda Briggs

## Splash

I also have happy memories of Harvey's roof garden café at Guildford, it was wonderful with frothy coffee in little glass cups, and we would sit on one of the 'islands' that the stepping stones in the photograph led to. I also remember my sister Sue being about 3 or 4 and falling in the pond head-first trying to touch the fish, Mum had to dry her out in the loo.

*Bob Whitehead*

Hindhead, Broom Squire's Cottage 1907 57877

## My great-grandfather Harvey Madgwick

*My great-grandfather, Harvey Madgwick, was a broom squire in the 1920s, and he lived in a cottage down in the 'bowl' (the Devil's Punch Bowl), as my mother related to me. It was a hard life for these people, but my mother (being brought up by her grandparents) told us many times of the broom squires and their children who lived there.*

Frances Hearn

'Broom squires' was the name given to people living in heathland areas who gathered heather, birch and brushwood to make besom brooms, an outdoor brush made from a bundle of twigs tied to a pole (like the 'flying broomstick' traditionally associated with witches). A number of people inhabiting the heathland around Hindhead used to make their living in this way. Besom brooms are still popular with gardeners, and are particularly good for sweeping away fallen leaves.

## Jonny 7

Back in the 1960s my sister used to take her dolls to the dolls' hospital in Swan Lane to get them fixed, they also mended teddy bears. My best memory of the dolls' hospital was that they used to have a 'Jonny 7' machine gun set up in the window, it was a toy gun that broke down into 7 different weapons. I was living on Bellfields then and my mum didn't have much money so she couldn't afford to buy me one. All of my mates were in the same boat, so we used to walk to town and spend ages looking through the shop window at it, as often as we could.

*Allen Nicol*

Guildford, Swan Lane c1955 G65173

# Kittens under the counter

As a child in the 1960s, I remember the staff in the Co-op store at South Merstham seen in this photograph asking me if I would like to see some kittens, which they produced from a cardboard box kept underneath the counter! The shop is now a hairdressers. The Morris Traveller car (registration XPD600) seen parked by the roadside outside the Co-op in this view belonged to my grandfather, Jack Deverill, who lived in Melton Road.

*Anthea Post*

South Merstham c1960 S665006

## Wartime memories

*I was born in 2 Pound Cottages in Hascombe in 1940. It was the home of my maternal grandparents Arthur John and Katie May Street. He was a gardener who worked for Colonel Harper at Lamberts. I recall a house in Godalming that was hit by a bomb and being embarrassed by furniture on view! There was a lone grave in what is now the churchyard extension at St Peter's of a German airman who had been found dead on Hascombe Hill. I am told that his body has since been returned to his family. Nurse Caines exercising her goats on their leads was a frequent sight if one were walking in the countryside. She ministered to me when my grandfather's terrier bit my wrist. I remember my grandfather made me a little wheelbarrow and small tools and the family stitched dungarees with seed packets attached to take part in a village fancy dress competition. A celebration was held at The Raswell for either VE or VJ day with fireworks and in my agitation I clasped the hand of a complete stranger! In those days, there was a second pub – the Royal Oak – in the centre of the village. My memories are of Ron and Molly Hoare running the White Horse and later I played with Rosemary, their daughter. My aunt, Vi Street, did domestic work at the pub on giving up her job at Dunsfold Aerodrome to look after her father when my grandmother died in 1950. The scene in this photo has changed little since it was taken in 1906. There is a wide sweep of car park opposite the White Horse as conservation area status has made the village a popular eating place and magnet for walkers and horse riders. Some of the pub's back garden has been surfaced as well. It is still the bus stop. The most striking change is the restoration of the pond by the church in memory of Daisy Coote, the dedicated schoolmistress. She always remembered my birthday which fell a day after her own on St George's Day even when my family moved away. In those days, Miss Musgrave who lived opposite the church was a terrifying lady to youngsters and once she caught me rearranging flowers in the churchyard, trying to share them with graves that had none! She played the organ for church services until she was very old. It is lovely that St Peter's Church has been restored so carefully – I can still recall the fishing net design on the walls of the nave in very poor and damp state.*

Jean Waddington

Hascombe, The White Horse 1906 53577

I was interested in your comments about Nurse Caines, who was the district nurse/midwife who assisted at my birth at Church Green, Dunsfold. She had to come out to me on her bicycle in the middle of a snowstorm – not too far in fact via Hookhouse Lane, since she lived at Loxhill. She later became my godmother, and as a small child after the war I was brought up on the milk from those goats of Nurse Caines!

*Mike Bayliss*

Oakwood Hill, Sent and Rydersfield Cottages 1906 53525

## Ryders folklore

These cottages are now known as Ryders, but it appears that in Edwardian times the place (or maybe this corner) may also have been known as 'Seven Trees Well': I have a postcard with this picture on it sent on 7th May 1906 to a Mr Jackson in Victoria Street, London; written on the reverse is 'Do you remember this place (7 tree well)....'. There is indeed a well here – just out of shot to the right. It is said that there is also a connection with the 1963 Great Train Robbery – a picture of some of the robbers standing in the garden once hung in the Punchbowl Inn up the road. (The area does have evidenced Train Robbery connections – £100,000 from the Robbery was found in Coldharbour Woods a few miles away.) The property was once owned by Rex Alston, a legendary BBC commentator in the 1950s and 60s. He co-presented some of the BBC coverage of the Coronation. The property also includes the old village forge, operated by Mr Holden (also of Ockley and Forest Green). Nearby is 'Ruckmans', a grand house designed by Lutyens with a magnificent tree-lined driveway flanked in spring by a spectacular mass of daffodils.

*Gary Crouch*

*It is said that there is also a connection with the 1963 Great Train Robbery – a picture of some of the robbers standing in the garden once hung in the Punchbowl Inn up the road.*

## Wartime Memories of Salfords

I started at Salfords School when I was about five around 1935. My first teacher was Miss Licence. Later I had Miss Kick and Miss Ferguson. There were no male teachers. The headmistress was Miss Atherton who had an Austin 7. My father would often take off her very deliberate hand signals. I was rather chatty in class and one of the punishments I was given was to be told to sit next to a lad who was known to be smelly! Can you imagine that! What must he have thought? I also sat next to Betty Springer. She was dark and very pretty but very conscious of being Jewish. I told her not to worry as I might be Jewish too! She was a good friend.

I lived in Siwah, Woodside Way, near to the school, where the Vance brothers Hughie and Bunny (Cyril) lived as well. Also in our 'gang' was Colin Oatridge, who often swore followed by 'God forgive me'. I thought we were destined for each other but he got a job as an undertaker and it put me off a bit. I also fell in love with Gordon Stevens. His father was a dustman but he had lovely wavy reddish hair. We used to go bird nesting in Pettridge Woods. We would blow the eggs and also collect bird skeletons. Colin Oatridge had a tent which we were all envious of and were very happy to play in with him when we got the chance.

Before the Second World War I remember there was a glow in the sky one night which my Dad, Cyril Hutchings, told me was Crystal Palace in south London burning down, in 1936.

When the war was imminent we had air-raid drills. We all had to shelter under the desks in the classroom. There was also a surface shelter in the play ground. However, when the war actually started we often had lessons in the Parish Hall because it was considered safer than the school itself. Many evacuees came from London and shared the school. For a period we attended in shifts and only went to school in the morning or afternoon. When invasion seemed imminent we expected German paratroopers would be landing. At school we were told that when they asked the way to London (it seemed to be presumed that this would be the only question they would ask!) we were to answer 'I cannot say'. We should not say 'I don't know', as that would be a lie. It might all seem ridiculous now but at the time we really thought that a German invasion was very likely.

One day during the Battle of Britain I was going across the common with my mother, Mary Hutchings, when some German bombers were intercepted by some Spitfire fighter planes. In the dogfight some of the bullets came down near us and my mother threw us down in a ditch and hid me under her arm. I distinctly remember her praying out loud. That was most unlike my mum, but it worked!

My dad built an air raid shelter in the back garden with reinforced concrete. He had served in the First World War so knew the power of explosives but comforted us by saying 'We'll be safe in here. Only a direct hit can get us now'. He worked at Hall & Co. where later in the war they serviced tanks. Sometimes he had to take his turn on fire-watching duty.

Salfords, The School 1907 57630

At the bottom of our garden was a farm which was run by Farmer Ginger. Sometimes the sheep came through the hedge into our garden and trampled everything, so my dad put up extra fencing. He also kept two allotments so we never went short of vegetables, but I did miss sweets which were on very short ration. When rationing started my mum said 'You can either have sugar in your tea but no jam or jam and no sugar in your tea'. So Dad and I said we would give up the sugar in our tea so we could continue to enjoy Mum's jam, especially blackberry and apple jelly.

Because of the war, in common with many others, we had to take lodgers. Some of them were workers from the local Monotype works, others were in service in Hapstead Hall, Ardingly. But we all socialised, playing cards and listening to the radio. I liked the extra company.

The war was sometimes a very frightening time for a child and the adults too, I am sure, but there was a great sense of camaraderie and there was often fun too, like singing and playing games in our air-raid shelter.

*Barbara Giles*

# Dancing to Bob Potter's band at The Atlanta

My name is Shirley Hamilton, maiden name Patten. I lived at Hammond Road, Horsell and as a teenager often danced at the Atlanta in Woking, it was the place to go, my friend Deirdre Jennings and I would sneak off on a Friday night. I remember it was like dancing in a giant goldfish bowl, the walls had fishes painted all around. Bob Potter was the attraction, he had a really good band. As I got older I became a hairstylist, doing my apprenticeship at Meads hairdressers and newsagents in Horsell. When I left there I was employed at the very top of the Atlanta on the left hand side of this picture in a hairdressers, and me and my colleague and friend Christine Campbell would hang out of the window in our lunch break to listen to Bob Potter and his band practicing, it was a great time for me. I have many happy memories as I am now 64, living in West Sussex but I was born in Woking and spent all my youth and thirties there, oh! happy days.

*Shirley Hamilton*

Woking, Public Hall 1902 48349

Reigate, Market Place and High Street 1939 88865

Reigate, Castle Caves, The Barons Hall 1886 18972

## Wartime Memories of Reigate, Doods Road, 1939-50

*In 1940, during the Second World War, my Granny and Grandad Weller, in their cramped semi in Doods Road in Reigate, took me, my mum and dad, my brother and sister plus 2 billeted soldiers under their loving wing, and I can honestly say that was the most happy household you could ever wish for. We knew things were serious when they installed concrete mini pyramids in the street outside which apparently would stop tanks from advancing. I also remember that people flocked to the 'safety' of Reigate Caves to sleep the night and shelter from air-raids, that was crazy on reflection because these are natural sand caves and I suspect one good wallop from a Doodle Bug that didn't get over the North Downs chalk cliffs would have caved the lot in, thank God it never happened. My father was an entertainer, a good one, highly professional in magic and ventriloquism (he won the UK International Brotherhood of Ventriloquism Cup in the 1950s). He trained me up at the age of 7 to carry out a 15 minute performance on any stage, doing magic using sleight of hand. I hated it but it meant that I did stand in front of 500 people in 1943 in Reigate Caves in full tail suit and patent leather shoes, entertaining people whilst Dorniers and Heinkels droned overhead.*

Norman Gardner

## Memories of the Basingstoke Canal at Frimley Green

I have many memories of the Basingstoke Canal at Frimley Green. I used to swim next to the Kingsmead Bridge. One day I was on the parapet of the bridge, I was grabbing a branch and swinging off the bridge. The branch broke and I hit the bridge wall below. I don't remember any more until I came round. Apparently I was knocked out. I came round and was pushed along by a soldier on a bike, wet through and fuzzy-headed – he saved my life. He told my mother everything, then he didn't give his name and left. I wish I had met him again, he certainly did me a favour. He could have been stationed at Deepcut, Pirbright, Blackdown or Mychett. I'm here today because of him. It was about the late 1940s.

I also remember the horse-drawn barges on the Basingstoke Canal at the Kings Head boat house and lock. The barges probably started from Aldershot, and went on through Surrey. I used to wait for the horse and walk under the bridge to the boat house. The bargeman would unhitch the horse and I would walk with them both to the King's Head pub, through a gate, turn left and up over the bridge to the lodge on the other side. I would hold the horse beside the lock. The bargeman would cross the lock, untie the rope and bring it back over. I felt really proud holding the bridle of the big horse. I never felt scared. The bargeman would hitch up and tow the barge through the lock, over the aquaduct and go on his way. The barges were huge, all wood, with just enough room to go through the locks – made to measure.

*Mr D R Richardson*

## Frimley Green during the Second World War

This is a memory of Frimley Green during the Second World War. My father, Samuel Fredrick Richardson, was the air-raid warden. There was a brick air-raid shelter built on the village green that most of the village used. One night we were in the shelter for almost the whole of the night, the air-raid went on for ages. In the early morning a Dornier bomber dropped bombs in the village – he had been shot down and needed to get rid of the bombs. My brother and his mate Johnny Hicks were in Wharf Road at the time,

Frimley, The Basingstoke Canal and New Boathouse 1909 61829p

and told us the story when we came out of the shelter. The pilot saw them and fired at them, and they dived into the ditch, and then the Dornier crashed into what we called the saw mills. Between Singleton's paper shop and the chemist's shop opposite the shelter was the allotment, which was demolished by one of the bombs dropped by the Dornier. The funny part (and not very nice for the chemist) was that the chemist was in his outside wooden toilet when the bomb fell, and blasted right next to him, blowing off the toilet door. We came out of the shelter to see him sitting on the toilet, knocked out by the blast, with his trousers round his ankles. There were a few chuckles from the mums. *Mr D R Richardson*

# Born in Prairie Road, Addlestone

I was born at 53 Prairie Road in 1964, my earliest memory is going to school in Chapel Park Infants School, Chapel Avenue, then we went up to the infants school in School Lane and then over the road to the juniors which I think used to be the boys school. I think at the time the new middle school was being built, and I eventually ended up at St Paul's middle school and on to the secondary school. I remember my mum taking me to get new school uniform to the Co-op and I was fascinated by the little tubes that they would put the money in and send it up the pipes and it would come back with your change and Co-op stamps. As a teenager I would spend many a happy hour 'up the town' and buying make-up in Woolworths or buying a single record in what I think was Spittles, I remember they used to cost about 50p. My mum worked in the launderette by the station next to a little cafe called Jane's Cafe, or was it called The Little Café? (My memory is not as good as used to be.) Then in the late 1970s there was a shop opened called Mr Flaks, and it was really trendy to get your jeans with huge flares from there. I also remember a sweet shop called 'Bon Bon', they sold the most amazing ice-creams in every different flavour. They were also up by the station. If I shut my eyes I can remember nearly every shop in Station Road and the High Street. It's sad to see how much it has changed and not really for the best.

*Helen Drawwater*

Addlestone, Station Road c1955 A23003

Addlestone, High Street 1954 A23021

## My Memories of Addlestone

*I remember going to fashion shows with a cup of tea and a biscuit in the Co-op in Addlestone on a Saturday. When I was younger the Co-op ran a sports day and we all got a goody box with cream cakes and a surprise of fruit. We shopped at Parrs at the top of the Duke's Head crossroads (seen on the left of this photograph), I can still remember the smell of the cured bacon. Our order was delivered by a man on a bike. Burges the bakers delivered our bread. We had our shoes repaired at Pigotts in Station Road and I went to both day school and boarding school with Dudly Piggot. We went to school on the bus from the bus garage and stood atop the bridge while the trains ran below and engulfed us in steam from the trains below. Airscrew and Weymonds were the biggest local employers. Traylens fun fair came to Addlestone every year, either the last week in July or the first in August. We got our meat from Chambers butchers and I remember Alma Chambers as Carnival Queen, I went to school with her sister Angela. I was the youngest of four children and my brother Mac played for Addlestone Football Club, my dad was the treasurer and my mum served teas on a match day.*

Sue Mackender

...my brother Mac played for Addlestone Football Club, my dad was the treasurer and my mum served teas on a match day.

## Thursley and the Sailor's Stone

*I grew up in Hindhead near Thursley in the 1960s and this story was extremely well known locally. On the walk which we did often up to Gibbet Hill above the Devil's Punch Bowl, you would pass the Sailor's Stone memorial which told the story of a horrible murder. The Sailor's Stone is still there, as is the unknown sailor's gravestone in Thursley churchyard which, having moved back to the area, I saw just the other day. The perpetrators met their victim in the Red Lion Inn, where they told him that they would keep him company on the road to Portsmouth. At Hindhead, then a bleak and almost uninhabited heath, they killed him and stripped him of all his possessions, rolling the body down into the Punch Bowl, where it was discovered the next morning by a local broom squire. The murderers were apprehended when they tried to sell the young sailor's clothes in a village further down the Portsmouth Road, and were tried, convicted and hanged in chains on the hill above the Punch Bowl, at 272 metres the second-highest point in Surrey. This hill, previously known as Butterwedge Hill, has been called Gibbet Hill ever since. Charles Dickens refers to the sailor's murder, which took place in 1786, in 'Nicholas Nickleby', when Nicholas and Smike come to Hindhead on their own journey down the Portsmouth Road, and Nicholas tells Smike the story related on the Sailor's Stone.*

Sally Partington

Hindhead, The Sailor's Stone and the Devil's Punch Bowl 1914 66707a

Thursley, The Churchyard, The Sailor's Gravestone 1902 48388

The murder of the sailor at Hindhead has indeed been a tale handed down from generation to generation. My brother was told about it by our dad, who in turn got it from his dad – indeed, if what my brother was told is correct, one of the three murderers was an ancestor of ours! Their names were: Lonergan, Casey and Marshall (Marshall's name was James). I have a copy of a trial document which I obtained from the National Archives and this prompted me to trace our family tree. As yet I have no definite proof that James Marshall was related to me but there is a strong possibility. Apparently only one of the murderers showed remorse for their crime and I like to think that it was James Marshall. I visited the graveyard at Thursley and found the sailor's stone and also visited Gibbet Hill. None of the murderers were buried – they were left on the gibbet until all that was left were bones which then turned to dust. Some might say a fitting end but I find it rather gruesome.

*Pauline Baldwin*

*– they were left on the gibbet until all that was left were bones...*

## One of my favourite fishing spots

This was one of my favourite fishing spots as a youngster in the 1950s. There used to be a bridge over the river here, but the bridge was blown up by the army around 1958. It was a fantastic sight and we rushed over to the river after the explosion to see all the dead fish.

*Paul Foster*

Hersham, The River Mole c1960 H398021

Redhill, Brighton Road c1955 R17026

## Watching the Olympic Torch carried through Redhill – for the 1948 London Olympics

*I was born in 1940 in Gillingham, Kent, my dad used to work for Short's, the aircraft builders. We moved to Redhill when I was a baby. One of my earliest memories was seeing the Olympic Torch runner coming down Redstone Hill in 1948, for the last time that the Olympics were held in London. I wonder if anyone can remember his name?*

*We also used to watch the Veteran Cars go through Redhill on the London to Brighton Car Run every year, as they still do, and on a Sunday evening in the summer we all used to go and watch the traffic jam coming back from the coast – we must have been hard up for entertainment! Mind you we didn't have a TV then!*

Bruce Cordy

Bletchingley, On Fair Day 1907 57493x

## The Small Boy on the Donkey...

*The small boy on the donkey in this photograph is my father, Arthur Wallis, who was born in 1904 in Bletchingley. The man standing to the right is my grandfather, Arthur Wallis senior, born 1862 in Bletchingley. Arthur Wallis senior was the licensee of the Red Lion Inn and later the proprietor of the newsagents in the background. The Wallis family came to Bletchingley in the early 1700s and for 200 years carried out bricklaying as their trade.*

Robert Wallis

# I used to come to Comerfords!

In October 1973 I bought my first motorbike from Comerfords in Thames Ditton (it would have been at top right of this picture, going along Portsmouth Road from Long Ditton); it was a Yamaha FS1e moped in 'Blackcurrant' metallic. But for up to two years earlier I would have cycled there from Hersham maybe 3 times a week to walk up and down the long isles of bikes or press my nose up against the window if on a Sunday. Across the road was also a little shop that had Puch mopeds – not the typical Maxi, but those rather eccentric two-toned bomb tank models. I desperately wanted a motorbike and the idea of having a friend ride pillion with me was so exciting. However, money for a teenager back then was difficult, so I did paper rounds, Saturday and holiday jobs to pay for it (at Bejams in Esher – now Iceland – and Waitrose in Weybridge) and eventually made my 16th birthday deadline and paid over my £179 for a brand new bike. I continued my efforts and also kept my moped in meticulous condition which enabled me to sell it for a small profit a year later. A year on, at the age of 17, I had a brand new Yamaha RD200 Twin (389) – the best motorcycle I have ever ridden! It was a blitzkrieg of a ride with masses of torque and hi revs. Then came girls and daily commutes to International Paint at Ham and a car seemed a good idea. Back to Comerfords who by now also sold Honda cars. I got an ex-demo, year-old Honda Civic 1200cc 3 door for £1,050 (it was less than half new price as it had 30,000 on the clock) and I learned and passed my test in it. I loved that place, but sadly all is now gone. I drove past for the first time in years in April 2010 and was stuck in the same old Portsmouth Road traffic I remembered! The pavement curb where I stood my pushbike all those years ago is all that looks the same... One last funny, the logbook for the FS1e declared the issuing dealer as Comesloads!

*Mark Gardiner*

Long Ditton, Portsmouth Road c1955 L457002

# Francis Frith

## Pioneer Victorian Photographer

Francis Frith, founder of the world-famous photographic archive, was a multi-talented man. A devout Quaker and a highly successful Victorian businessman, he was philosophical by nature and pioneering in outlook. By 1855 he had already established a wholesale grocery business in Liverpool, and sold it for the astonishing sum of £200,000, which is the equivalent today of over £15,000,000. Now in his thirties, and captivated by the new science of photography, Frith set out on a series of pioneering journeys up the Nile and to the Near East.

He was the first photographer to venture beyond the sixth cataract of the Nile. Africa was still the mysterious 'Dark Continent', and Stanley and Livingstone's historic meeting was a decade into the future. The conditions for picture taking confound belief. He laboured for hours in his wicker dark-room in the sweltering heat of the desert, while the volatile chemicals fizzed dangerously in their trays. Back in London he exhibited his photographs and was 'rapturously cheered' by members of the Royal Society. His reputation as a photographer was made overnight.

By the 1870s the railways had threaded their way across the country, and Bank Holidays and half-day Saturdays had been made obligatory by Act of Parliament. All of a sudden the working man and his family were able to enjoy days out, take holidays, and see a little more of the world.

With typical business acumen, Francis Frith foresaw that these new tourists would enjoy having souvenirs to commemorate their days out. For the next thirty years he travelled the country by train and by pony and trap, producing fine photographs of seaside resorts and beauty spots that were keenly bought by millions of Victorians. These prints were painstakingly pasted into family albums and pored over during the dark nights of winter, rekindling precious memories of summer excursions. Frith's studio was soon supplying retail shops all over the country, and by 1890 F Frith & Co had become the greatest specialist photographic publishing company in the world, with over 2,000 sales outlets, and pioneered the picture postcard.

Francis Frith had died in 1898 at his villa in Cannes, his great project still growing. By 1970 the archive he created contained over a third of a million pictures showing 7,000 British towns and villages.

Frith's legacy to us today is of immense significance and value, for the magnificent archive of evocative photographs he created provides a unique record of change in the cities, towns and villages throughout Britain over a century and more. Frith and his fellow studio photographers revisited locations many times down the years to update their views, compiling for us an enthralling and colourful pageant of British life and character.

We are fortunate that Frith was dedicated to recording the minutiae of everyday life. For it is this sheer wealth of visual data, the painstaking chronicle of changes in dress, transport, street layouts, buildings, housing and landscape that captivates us so much today, offering us a powerful link with the past and with the lives of our ancestors.

Computers have now made it possible for Frith's many thousands of images to be accessed almost instantly. The archive offers every one of us an opportunity to examine the places where we and our families have lived and worked down the years. Its images, depicting our shared past, are now bringing pleasure and enlightenment to millions around the world a century and more after his death. For further information visit: www.francisfrith.com

# Index of Photographs

# Francis Frith Products & Services

Francis Frith would doubtless be pleased to know that the pioneering publishing venture he started in 1860 still continues today. Over a hundred and forty years later, The Francis Frith Collection continues in the same innovative tradition and is now the foremost publisher of vintage photographs in the world. Some of the current products and activities include:

## FRITH PRINTS

All Frith photographs are available in a range of print sizes and formats, including mounted, framed and on canvas. Customers may choose from over 120,000 images on the Frith web site.

## FRITH BOOKS

The Francis Frith Collection has published over 1,100 books, including many local histories of towns, counties and regions. See the web site for a complete list of those currently available.

## GIFT PRODUCTS

Other products published by Frith include local Calendars, Postcards, Personalised Jigsaws and Historical Maps centred on any address in the UK.

## INTERIOR DECOR

Today Frith's photographs can be seen framed and as giant wall murals in thousands of pubs, restaurants, hotels, banks, retail stores and other public buildings throughout the country. In every case they enhance the unique local atmosphere of the places they depict and provide reminders of gentler days in an increasingly busy and frenetic world.

## GENEALOGY AND FAMILY HISTORY

As the interest in family history and roots grows world-wide, more people are turning to Frith for images of the towns, villages and streets where their ancestors lived. Photographs of the churches and chapels where ancestors were christened, married and buried are an essential part of every genealogy tree and family album.

## REMINISCENCE THERAPY

Historical photographs are recognized to be beneficial in stimulating the memory of the elderly and those with dementia. Frith photographs are used as décor in care and residential homes and in reminiscence therapy software.

## PHOTO LIBRARY

Frith images are regularly licensed to other publishers & manufacturers for use in their own products.

## PRODUCT PROMOTIONS

Frith products have been used by many major companies to promote the sales of their own products or to reinforce their own history and heritage.

Mounted Prints

Framed Prints

Books

Historical Maps

## SHARE YOUR FAMILY MEMORIES

We hope this book will have sparked memories of your own. Why not take a moment to remember the places that have been important in your life - where your family comes from, where you were born, went to school or married; the towns and villages where you've lived and worked since. Recapture and rekindle those precious memories by visiting our web site and enjoy browsing over 120,000 historical photographs of British towns and villages. Simply visit our web site and search for your favourite places. While you are there why not read some of the thousands of memories contributed by other visitors and then share your own at: **www.francisfrith.com**

Prints on Canvas

Jigsaws

Calendars

## THE FRANCIS FRITH COLLECTION

Oakley Business Park, Wylye Road,
Dinton, Wiltshire SP3 5EU, England.
Telephone: **01722 716 376** Fax: **01722 716 881**
email: **sales@francisfrith.co.uk**
**www.francisfrith.com**



## Frith Shop 15% Discount Code

If you have enjoyed this book you may wish to purchase other products from The Francis Frith Collection.

As a returning customer we would like to offer you a **15% discount** off your next order.

You may redeem this voucher by post, mail or telephone, or on our website simply by quoting the unique Voucher Code below:

### Your 15% voucher code:

**FRITH15**

### to redeem your voucher:

**Visit our website: www.francisfrith.com** and enter the Voucher Code at the Checkout.

**By Mail:** Write with details of your order quoting the Voucher Code and deducting 15% from your payment (excluding the P&P charge).

**By Phone:** Call 01722 716 376 to talk to our knowledgeable staff and quote your Voucher Code.

**Small Print:** The 15% discount will be applied to your order value (excluding Post & Packing charges) and may be redeemed at any time – there is no end date. This offer only applies to orders placed directly with The Francis Frith Collection and is subject to the limitations detailed above. This offer does not apply to trade customers. Please note this offer is limited to one order only (per customer/delivery address) and may not be combined with any other offer.

**DELIVERIES OUTSIDE THE UK**
See our website for details of products and deliveries overseas.

**GUARANTEE OF QUALITY** We are confident that you will be completely satisfied with any Frith product. If for any reason you are unhappy with your purchase, simply return it within 30 days for a full refund of your purchase price.

Voucher litho